HEROIC DOGS

To Iain Gordon

*Also to the glorious English
setters – Sophie, Carol, Sweet 'n
Tiddly, Cindy, Sukie, Lady, Poppy
and Fanta; and including the
Cockers Dixie and Ella*

HEROIC DOGS

Lesley Scott-Ordish

Arlington Books
Bury St, St James's
London

HEROIC DOGS
First published 1990 by
Arlington Books (Publishers) Ltd
Distributed by Biblios Ltd
Horsham

© Lesley Scott-Ordish 1990

British Library Cataloguing in Publication Data
Scott-Ordish. Lesley
Heroic Dogs.
1. Livestock: Dogs. Relationships with man.
I. Title
636.7
ISBN 0-85140-787-0

Typeset by Inforum Typesetting, Portsmouth
Printed and bound in Great Britain by
Biddles Ltd, Guildford

Contents

Acknowledgements

Thanks to all who assisted work and research in compiling this book, and the following for allowing the use of copyright photographs: Sally Anne Thompson, Phil Drabble, Mercury Press, *The Times*, *Dog World* Publications, Irene Matthews, *Kent Messenger*, *Daily Mirror*, *Daily Telegraph*, Doreen Vincent, *Northampton Mercury*, James Tolleth, Roy J Sabine, Grayling Company, Metropolitan Police, H.M. Customs and Excise, David Dalton, Vic Keith, *Leicester Mercury*, Albert Gibbons, Surrey and South London Newspapers, Sue Holleron, *Daily Star*, Bonita Whitfield.

Thanks to Jilly Cooper for her help and encouragement in an hour of need and to Doreen Vincent for her painstaking hours of photography given to assist the publication of this book.

This book is written to assist the work of the PRO Dogs National Charity, registered number 275574, which the author founded in 1976 and of which she is still the honorary Director. The President of the charity is HSH Princess Antoinette of Monaco and there is a qualified medical, veterinary and legal advisory panel under the Chairmanship of Andrew Bowden MBE, MP. The charity operates throughout Britain from Scotland to the Channel Isles, with overseas connections, and has a membership voice of over 20,000.

PRO Dogs works to promote the benefits of dogs to society and to ensure, through its growing membership, caring standards both of breeding and ownership. The aim is for dogs to be wanted and appreciated, not only as amazingly adaptable domestic animals but also for the benefits which medical science is beginning to understand, which come about as a result of the bond between people and companion animals. All this at a time when slaughter of the huge excess of unwanted dogs in the world is the order of the day.

For further information about the work of the charity, how to join as a member, or take part in the Pets As Therapy hospital visiting scheme, please be kind enough to send s.a.e. to:

PRO Dogs National Charity, Department HD, Rocky Bank, 4 New Road, Ditton, Aylesford, Kent ME20 6AD

Roll of Honour
PRO Dog of the Year Gold Medal Awards

		WINNERS	JUDGES
1979	SANDY	Labrador retriever: For saving the life of Darren Connor, aged 17, in difficulties in the River Thames: Life Saving	Brian Imber Maureen Shelley Jean Spendley Clarisse Charlton
	RATS	Mongrel dog of corgi proportions: For bravery, devotion to duty and the comfort provided to soldiers serving in Crossmaglen: Devotion to Duty	Jennifer Heard Lesley Scott-Ordish
	TANSY	Golden retriever: For being a canine blood donor and saving the life of a West Highland White Terrier: Pet of the Year	
1980	DOUGAL	Pekingese: For rousing Mrs Clare Sheldon and her daughter Julie, in danger of death from carbon monoxide poisoning: Life Saving	Iain Gordon Maureen Shelley Clarisse Charlton Brian Imber
	EMMA	Chocolate coloured Labrador: A trained working guide dog for the blind, who lost her own sight while serving her owner: Devotion to Duty	Lesley Scott-Ordish
	KALLI	Cross bred Collie bitch: For her strong maternal instinct which led her to feed and rear many orphan animals including a lion, tiger, puma and two Artic fox cubs: Pet of the Year	
1981	LASKA	Samoyed: For saving the life of 81 year old Norman Stephenson, when he fell to the bottom of an embankment: Life Saving	Brian Imber Iain Gordon Maureen Shelley Lesley Scott-Ordish
	DANDYDEER FRANZ	German Shepherd police dog: For two incidents, involving searching and finding an elderly man and a lost young child in course of duty: Devotion to Duty	

	GOLDIE	Golden retriever from the BBC television programme *Blue Peter*: For being a much loved substitute pet for many children, unable to have a dog of their own: Pet of the Year	
1982	ZAK	Dobermann: For saving 11 year old David Dudding from death by drowning when he got into difficulties at sea: Life Saving	Ivan Spencer Iain Gordon Nigel O'Nions Ray Owen
	BRUMBY	Labrador retriever bred by the Guide Dog for the Blind Association and passed on to HM Customs and Excise Investigation division because of his great exuberence: For a record 210 successful drug detections worth over £4m: Devotion to Duty	Len Pearce Maureen Shelley Lesley Scott-Ordish
	BOTHIE	Terrier, the intrepid North and South Pole travelling companion dog: For comfort and companionship in extreme conditions: Pet of the Year	
1983	TRIPPER	Collie dog: For perseverance in saving the life of his handicapped owner, Jim Rigg, when he collapsed with an epileptic fit on the Gower coast as the tide was coming in: Life Saving	Ivan Spencer Iain Gordon Andrew Ferry Bob Jones Suzanne Simon Lesley Scott-Ordish
	JET	Labrador retriever: For courage and persistence in mountain rescue resulting in a large number of successful rescue missions: Devotion to Duty	
	MICKY	Jack Russell terrier: For saving the life of Percy the Chihuahua who had been buried alive: Pet of the Year	
1984	JUDY	Jack Russell terrier: for saving the life of her 74 year old crippled owner, Joseph Bennett, when fire broke out in their home: Life Saving	
	KHAN	German Shepherd police dog who apprehended two suspects, despite severe internal injuries after being run down by a car: Devotion to Duty	

	SANDY	Sandy coated mongrel: For causing so much fun by learning to climb a ladder to be a window cleaner's mate: Pet of the Year	
1985	TOBY	Dachshund-type mongrel: For saving ten human lives by his insistence in raising the alarm following a major gas leak in Basingstoke: Life Saving	Ivan Spencer Iain Gordon Roy Cox Bob Jones Suzanne Simon Lois Cowdery Lesley Scott-Ordish
	NIPPER	The Collie: For bravery in overcoming the danger and fear of fire to rescue his sheep: Devotion to Duty	
	OSCAR	German Wirehaired Pointer: For causing great amusement as a 'Newshound' and raising many thousands of pounds for charity: Pet of the Year	
1986	HARVEY	Basset Hound: For raising the alarm when fire broke out in his home in Launceston after the family had retired to bed and saving the lives of 5 year old Leah and her mother Mrs Sandra Kramer: Life Saving	Iain Gordon Brian Imber Bob Jones Peter Keyte Leslie Dickson Lesley Scott-Ordish
	FAVOUR	Crossbreed: For being the first dog trained in Britain and chosen by Hearing Dogs for the Deaf to demonstrate the benefits of dogs for people with hearing loss: Devotion to Duty	
	SCHNORBITZ	St Bernard, by popular demand: For being such a well known and lovable dog: Pet of the Year	
1987	LOCH	Border Collie from the English Mountain Rescue scheme: For saving life after the El Salvador earthquake disaster: Life Saving	Ivan Spencer Iain Gordon Bob Jones David Levy Kandy Bate Lesley Scott-Ordish
	MEG	Border Collie from the Welsh Mountain Rescue team: For work to assist the El Salvador earthquake disaster: Devotion to Duty	
	JACOB	Long coat German Shepherd: For bravery and intelligence in returning his owner's bag from a mugger: Pet of the Year	

1988	MAX	Mongrel: For bravely stopping the kidnap of his 11 year old owner Vicky Clark: Life Saving	Ivan Spencer Iain Gordon David Levy Dick Taplin Lesley Scott-Ordish
	SAMMY	German Shepherd dog: For bravery in protecting her owner from a rogue horse, at the cost of the loss of her right eye: Devotion to Duty	
	JAMES	Corgi: For being a dog of Royal breeding working as a hospital visiting P.A.T. Dog: Pet of the Year	
1989	PASHA	German Shepherd dog: For saving the life of his owner Nikola Stedul from a would be assassin: Life Saving	Ivan Spencer Iain Gordon Bob Jones David Levy Dick Taplin Michaela Edridge Lesley Scott-Ordish
	JASON	Black Labrador: For saving the lives of 4 soldiers by detecting and warning of a bomb, despite injury to himself: Devotion to Duty	
	BOO	For drawing attention to a cancerous mole on the leg of her owner Mrs Bonita Whitfield, leading to treatment at the curable stage, and raising interest in the possible future use of dogs to detect melanomas: Pet of the Year	

Foreword

How refreshing it is to read a book devoted solely to *good* dogs, when the press and media run incessant campaigns to convince us that the British are no longer a nation of dog lovers!

There are, of course, *no* bad dogs. Only bad owners. Lesley Scott-Ordish has not only written a delightful book which proves the point but, because she *cares* so much about what really is Man's best friend, she will inspire countless others to emulate her.

I learned, first hand, about the therapeutic quality of a dog as a boon companion when my mother died just before my ninth birthday.

My father gave me Mick, a mongrel bull-terrier to try to ease my loss and he was my shadow for the next ten years.

Together we learned the arts of ferreting for rats; we went for endless country walks; no bullyboy dared bully me and, when our day was done, he spent his nights at the foot of my bed.

Since those days, I have felt half dressed without a dog and among the greatest joys which dogs have conferred on me is introducing me to fellow dog owners.

I am lucky enough now to work in lovely country places, with delightful people and I know, from experience, just how good a well behaved dog is as an introduction to kindred spirits.

Walk into a country pub, with a well mannered dog at your heels, and the betting is that before you have swallowed a drink, someone will ask 'Is he any good, then?' Not 'is he pretty?', or 'has he won any prizes?', but just 'is he any good?' They want to know if he is the sort of dog which the author has starred in this delightful book.

Everyone knows what invaluable work – and such '*work*' is sheer pleasure to a dog! – the Guide Dogs for the Blind have been doing for years. Lesley Scott-Ordish here highlights the equally vital job they do by being the ears, on four legs, for the deaf.

But it is relatively recently, and in no small measure due to the

1. *Phil Drabble, author of many books and presenter of the popular BBC television series,* One Man and His Dog, *on his wildlife preserve with his German shorthaired pointer Tick and Alsation Belle.*

author's crusading work, that the medical profession has realised how very comforting it is to old people, who may have been forced through incapacity, to move to residential homes, to be visited by a dog, which accepts and befriends them as if they were its own pack leader.

Having been involved with the television sheep dog programme *One Man and His Dog* for the last fifteen years, it has been my privilege to meet a great many farmers and shepherds, who spend a large part of their working lives in the solitude of wild hills, with only a dog for companion. I choose the term *only* deliberately to highlight the fact that no other companion could supply so many needs.

They work so closely together, shepherding their sheep, that they achieve a truly telepathic relationship, for a good collie seems to be able to read their shepherd's thoughts before he has time to translate them into commands.

Tens of thousands of acres of wonderful hill country would revert to scrub without the help of working sheep dogs, because no mechanical contrivance could negotiate the precipitous sheep walks to drive the flock where it was wanted.

Without a *working* sheep dog, of the type referred to in this book, it would be impossible to rescue stock buried in snowdrifts and the mountain rescue service rely heavily on such dogs.

Lesley Scott-Ordish has collected a magnum of Heroic Dogs in her book. I am certain that it will inspire men and women of good will to emulate her example by telling the world that such dogs are a gift to treasure.

Introduction: unrecognised heroes

Dogs live to please their owners.

So often, dogs are frustrated in their natural desire to live with other dogs, and people become their substitute companions to be served and pleased at all costs.

The trouble is the difficulty which modern man has in understanding animals so that we are able to recognise the worth of animal sacrifice in living with us.

It has always been a considerable challenge to sensitive people to get through the communication barrier so that we can 'talk' to animals, or at least learn to live with them to our mutual contentment and satisfaction.

In some ways, early man may have managed this rather better than his civilised counterpart. But even today many people have not forgotten the urge to use the highly developed instincts of animals for our own advantage in hunting and for pleasure and to do so in a way which is equally rewarding for the animal.

In the highly human-populated lands in which we live, we are relying on domestic animals to fill a growing number of our needs.

Of all domestic animals, dogs are the most adaptable. What other animal is there which –

gives protection and companionship to people

guides the blind

is trained to help the deaf

is regularly used on therapy visits to hospitals and homes for the elderly

assists the hill farmer and the shepherd

works for the police

is trained for the armed forces

is employed by H M Customs and Excise to sniff out drugs

and provides endless fulfilling leisure hours in competitive events, such as breed and obedience competitions, agility events, greyhound racing and many other country pursuits?

The list is far from complete, but gives some idea of the astonishing range of services which dogs are called upon to provide for the benefit of people.

I

BRAVE BREED DOGS

2. *Jacob, the intelligent German shepherd dog who retrieved this handbag after it had been snatched by a mugger, and returned it to Betty Harris, his owner.*

1. *Debagging the thief*

Intelligent dogs can be trained to a remarkably high degree, but there has always been argument as to whether dogs can think and reason for themselves.

The cold scientific view is usually that acts of heroism in animals can be dismissed as purely instinctive, or carried out for self protection of the animal.

Many carefully researched accounts of bravery by dogs in this book show that dogs often act way outside the strong basic survival need of self protection and that dogs sometimes face up to terrifying situations in order to protect or defend their owners or the property of their owners.

A German shepherd dog called Jacob, reported in *The Daily Telegraph* and other UK National papers in January 1987, will provide an interesting illustration.

Jacob had been sent by his owner, Mrs Betty Harris, on a 'down stay' obedience exercise some distance away from her in a field of long grass. For this exercise, dogs are required to stay lying down, until called again by the handler.

Whilst waiting, the dog saw his owner punched and robbed by a mugger who then ran off with her handbag. Without any further command from his owner, who turned in distress and ran home in panic to her husband Michael, the dog set off in pursuit, forcing the thief to surrender his haul.

Within minutes, Jacob arrived at the family's home in Sandrock Road, Wallasay, Merseyside, carrying Mrs Harris's stolen shoulder bag in his mouth. The contents were intact, but the dog was bleeding from his mouth.

Betty Harris had been frightened and winded, but not hurt and recovered quickly with delight when she saw Jacob. 'I couldn't believe it when Jacob came trotting in with the bag. He looked so proud of himself, and it was so clever of him to go and get it back for me.'

The police immediately started investigations, but the offender was never brought to book. The quick action of the dog may nevertheless have given the thief a sharp surprise and a useful lesson.

Jacob is one of very many dogs nominated for the increasingly sought after 'Canine Oscars'. These are gold medal awards presented on a ribbon for the dog to wear round its neck at an annual awards night for dogs.

Anxious to counter growing intolerance to dogs in society, the national PRO Dogs charity invites nominations for three medals which are presented annually in the following categories (if the standard is sufficiently high). There is one each for life saving, devotion to duty and pet of the year.

The life saving award goes to a dog which has either unquestionably saved human life, or made a contribution to the saving of human life.

The devotion to duty medal usually goes to a dog which is trained in the service of people (such as perhaps police dogs, drug detection dogs or dogs trained to assist handicapped people) but which has acted beyond normal expectations or demands.

Pet of the year is the fun category and allows anyone and everyone who thinks their dog deserves a medal to apply. Well known dogs from stage or television have been popular also in this category because they often become so loved as 'substitute' dogs by people unable to have a dog of their own. Dogs who have made an unusual contribution as a family pet, and draw attention to the diverse ways dogs captivate and entertain us, sometimes win this award.

It has been my pleasure to be involved with these awards ever since they were introduced in 1978.

Nominations pour in throughout the year and close each year on 30 September. A short list of the most deserving and unusual is then made for the judging panel and preliminary research begins.

It helps if the police have been notified and involved in the incident, or any other of the emergency services. The work of research is quite complex and as many facts as possible need to be included to substantiate the evidence. Most nominations fail because they cannot be sufficiently proved.

Eventually two candidates are left in each category and the owners notified – and sworn to secrecy!

The announcement of the final winners is not made to the Press Association until noon of the day of the awards dinner, usually held in December. By this time anticipation is considerable and excitement intense.

When first these awards were suggested by Brian Imber, a member of PRO Dogs, there was concern in case dogs did not generate enough good deeds in a year to merit them. What would happen if suddenly there were no reports about life-saving dogs? The charity did not want to launch a short-term project with little chance of building it up to an interesting annual event.

Doubts proved unjustified. Dogs did not disappoint. Each year it seems that more and more activities are considered for awards. And behind every one of them is benefit for people – even if it's only a jolly good laugh at some amazing antic from a pet dog, or a report in the medical press about the keen scenting ability of a dog which has led to detection of a life-threatening tumour. (See page 147).

For practical reasons, the PRO Dogs medals are confined to dogs resident in the U.K. Otherwise dogs would need to spend six months in quarantine kennels on entry to Britain to comply with current rabies laws.

The medals are also confined to living animals, rather than dogs which have been killed in saving their owners. The dog has to be included in the celebration and be there to wear the medal round his neck. This gives vital photographs and good press cover to promote the status of dogs in society and encourage higher standards of ownership.

It is hoped this will to some extent counter the media hype about dangers and risks from dogs, which leads to large numbers of dogs being abandoned and ever more unwanted dogs.

Jacob certainly received a good response to the report of his award, including a personal letter from the Chairman of British Airways, The Lord King of Wartnaby, enclosing a new bag to replace the one which was blood-stained in the snatch.

Following this remarkable retrieve, Jacob received his gold medal award as pet of the year in 1987. The citation reads: For bravery and intelligence in returning his owner's bag, from a mugger.

—— DID YOU KNOW? ——

Wanted: Deaf dog

In dog rescue, there are always more dogs than suitable homes to be found.

Although there is regular demand for small bitches, house-trained and appealing young dogs or pedigree pups at non-pedigree prices, the old or difficult dog waits and waits. Usually in vain.

So when an elderly gentleman came in one day and asked to be put on the waiting list for a deaf dog, it was a welcome surprise.

Deaf dogs present almost insuperable problems for the unwary, and of course we enquired why it had to be deaf.

'Well,' he said, 'I've just lost my old dog Sally. She was deaf and it took a long time for us to understand each other. But I know how to do it now and it's satisfying when they learn to look and respond to hand signals.

'Now I know the secret, I want to try and help another dog like that'.

As most caring breeders put down pups as soon as it is discovered that they are deaf, so as not to risk carrying on a line which produces such a serious defect, he had some time to wait. But we found him one in the end.

2. *Saving a stranger*

It is not unknown for a dog to arrive at a specialist breed rescue society in such a low state that it wants only to starve itself to death.

Such a dog was the beautiful two and a half year old Samoyed, Laska. Her elderly first owner had died suddenly, and Laska was pining for him.

The only way to save the life of a dog in such a situation is to find a patient new owner quickly. If you can also add a new interest to life with a bit of competition at mealtimes, so much the better.

Largely thanks to the concern of devoted Samoyed owners David and Wendy Lawson, Laska was fortunate. She went to live with the Richardson family in Rastrick, Brighouse, Yorkshire. The competition came in the form of a five year old Samoyed called Emma, already in residence. And it worked.

For just about twelve months, Laska lived a life of contentment with the Richardsons and Emma. And then, suddenly, one evening she disappeared through the garden gate which had been left open by one of the children.

Consternation and a five hour organised search failed to find her on that cold wet night in late September, 1981. The police had received no report of a dog handed in, and at last the family went to bed.

Eight miles away near Great Horton, Bradford, the police were involved in another search. Mary Stephenson had reported that her rather forgetful eighty-one year old husband was also missing. The hour was late, the weather bad and he had gone off without his coat. Despite the night search, he could not be found.

Next day the search continued. But eventually the frail Mr Norman Stephenson was discovered by chance, where he had fallen unconscious at the bottom of an embankment in a field at Hipperholme, some 4.5 miles (78.24km) from his home. And there snuggled up to protect him was Laska who had by some amazing

3. *Laska the Samoyed who won the PRO Dog of the Year gold medal for saving the life of eighty-one-year-old Mr Norman Stephenson. This elderly man was out all night in bad weather, having fallen to the bottom of an embankment.*

chance, or instinct, found him and stayed with him through his sixteen hour ordeal. Two men out walking found the two together, about mid-way between the homes of man and dog.

Mr Stephenson was taken at once to hospital, suffering from exposure, but made a gradual recovery. He was full of gratitude for Laska when his wife Mary visited him and was photographed with the cuddly white dog on many occasions when the national press picked up the unusual story.

Police Superintendent David Carter said at Brighouse Police Station that he believed the old man would undoubtedly have died, if the dog had not stayed and provided the critical warmth and protection.

Laska's Russian ancestors had the same protective instinct for their owners when the breed was used as sledge and herding dogs. The breed is well known for its faithful nature and Samoyeds have been known to keep their masters alive in sub-zero temperatures by wrapping themselves around them.

Wendy Lawson, who reported the deed to PRO Dogs for consideration of an award said:

'We often hear of dogs saving their own masters, but this was a stranger. This deed must surely be worthy of an award.'

We may never completely understand how it was that Laska homed in on Norman Stephenson in his hour of need, but when she had found him she may have had her great affection for her original master aroused, possibly by a similarity in body smell by which dogs recognise people at the deepest level.

Laska was presented with the 1981 PRO Dog of the year gold medal award for lifesaving in London, where there was great celebration with a champagne reception followed by the annual dinner.

In researching the story for this book, I discovered that following a separation in her second home, Laska returned to David and Wendy Lawson, who had been so concerned for her welfare earlier.

There she had more Samoyeds to live with and settled into a happy life, where she was much loved. Despite being rather a light-boned dog compared with her more substantial companions, she kept up with the best of them and surpassed them in stamina.

She died on the night of Sunday 13 August, 1989 at the age of nearly twelve years, but will certainly live on in the memory of those who knew or read about her.

4. *Laska receives her gold medal from the author, with Mrs Sue Richardson and Mr Easson of Wilson's of Dundee, who supported the first years of these awards.*

DID YOU KNOW?

Breed Rescue Societies

Nearly every recognised breed of dog now has its own breed 'rescue' organisation in America, Britain and some other European countries, at least.

These groups have a good knowledge of the different instincts and needs of their breed and are best placed to rehome dogs when it unfortunately becomes necessary to do so.

The higher divorce statistics, with split up of families, often means parting with a dog. Many of the breed rescue groups are registered charities or non profit organisations and worth contacting and supporting.

3.   Blood-donor dog

Bravery of a different kind comes from animals volunteered by their owners to give some sort of benefit to others. In this situation, the animal has no free choice but deserves to be recognised for the manner in which it behaves under possibly stressful conditions.

Golden retrievers (and, indeed, most of the gun dog group of dogs) as well as greyhounds, are perhaps notable for their long-suffering nature and some might even be described as stoic.

Tansy a golden retriever was one such dog.

One morning in September 1979, veterinary surgeon Tony Hardwick had to perform a life saving operation on Ceilidh, a small West Highland white terrier. But the little dog suffered a haemorrhage following surgery and was in danger of bleeding to death.

What was Tony Hardwick to do? In Britain there was no blood transfusion service for dogs and no covering service to call upon. Without a replacement of lost blood very quickly, the Westie would be lost.

Next door to the surgery in Chichester, West Sussex, lived another patient to the veterinary surgery, Tansy and owner Mrs Irene Matthews.

Tansy was known to the vet as a gentle tolerant dog. She was fit and healthy and about five years of age. There was no doubt that she could easily spare up to a pint of blood without ill effect. But how would Irene Matthews respond to a request for her much loved dog to be used for such a purpose? Was it even ethical to ask a client to subject their dog to what would be something of an experimental procedure, with no guarantee that the life of the Westie would definitely be saved? Certainly there would be no time for cross-matching the blood, to ensure compatibility. Indeed, in dogs, a first transfusion of blood can be certain not to cause a matching problem in about ninety per cent of dogs.

All these thoughts must have raced through the head of the vet

5. *Tansy the canine blood donor called on by vet Tony Hardwick to save the life of a small West Highland white terrier.*

as in spite of his intensive efforts he watched as Ceilidh grew weaker and weaker.

His mind was made up. He had to ask, and he dashed round to see Irene Matthews. The good lady hesitated only long enough to understand the full implication of the request as Tony Hardwick patiently explained. Tansy looked up at him with trusting eyes and wagged her tail as she walked off with him.

Swiftly the hair was shaved off Tansy's leg to make it easier to find the vein, while Helen the nurse spoke reassuringly to her. As large a needle as the vein could easily accommodate was inserted, and the life-giving fluid gradually withdrawn. Tansy lay peacefully, not adding to the tense situation in the surgery.

Quite soon the contribution was large enough to start injecting with a smaller needle into the limp body of the Westie.

At first, no visible signs of improvement could be seen. But then gradually the heart-beat of the little dog started to return to normal and her pulse and breathing improved. She became warmer as life seemed to flow back into her again.

The vet and the nurse took a deep breath of relief. Ceildih was going to live.

Tansy was returned none the worse to her white-faced owner, who had probably suffered as much as anyone in the ordeal. Her dog meant so much to her, that she asked herself continually if she had really done the right thing – until she saw her happy dog safely returned.

Mrs Matthews says that the incident became something of a turning point in her own life. Her eyes had been opened to ways in which dogs can help and she was so proud of her dog that she nominated Tansy for one of the PRO Dog of the Year awards. She also worked to promote Tansy's good image by collecting money for various good causes, which the local papers were only too pleased to report.

Tansy received the award for Pet of the Year in December 1979 and was invited to take part in the British major dog show Cruft's, in the personality parade the following February. Tansy was now famous and nothing could have given her owner greater pleasure.

It seems that Tansy was the first blood donor dog to receive substantial press cover for her contribution and this may have encouraged others.

The most usual source of blood for emergency use is provided by dogs belonging to vets or veterinary nurses. They are conveniently to hand and suffer less stress in the hands of people they know well. These dogs are used quietly and as often as needed for

6. *Holly the cocker spaniel with a rare blood disease, whose need for emergency transfusions encouraged her owners to set up a register of dog blood donors in Britain. Here seen promoting a stamp fund-raising campaign.*

emergencies, usually following road traffic accidents or the removal of tumours causing considerable blood loss.

A Great Dane/greyhound cross owned by Mrs Marion Green who works at the Royal Veterinary College in Hertfordshire, England, deserves an honourable mention.

Twizzle is a large placid dog who has been called upon on numerous occasions by veterinary surgeon Dr Serena Brownlie at the Royal College where complex cases and cases of a specialized nature are referred. Large dogs can obviously spare more blood than small ones, and Twizzle is so tolerant that between the years of 1983–89, he has provided a total of twelve pints taken from the jugular vein in his neck.

In 1986, a red cocker spaniel named Holly was referred to the college at the age of eight months when bleeding of the dog's gums did not stop naturally following loss of a puppy tooth. It seemed that the dog had a form of haemophilia, but investigation showed that for some reason the dog had an abnormally low blood platelet count which prevented clotting.

Holly had lost so much blood that Dr Brownlie quickly arranged a transfusion from her own Samoyed dog to save the young dog's life.

Subsequently Holly needed another transfusion three years later and this time a dobermann called Cass from the medical department of the college provided the necessary service.

Harry Hibben, the owner of Holly, was deeply grateful for the personal use of dogs owned by staff members to twice save the life of his own dog and determined to show his gratitude in a positive way.

He set out to introduce and maintain a computer register of large and healthy dogs, aged between two and ten years of age whose owners would volunteer to provide them as blood donors for emergency use throughout England.

People are quick to answer the call for human donors and, once the need is recognised, there is no reason why there should not be a good response from dog owners.

It is surprising how many initiatives for the benefit of animals seem to have started in Kent, England. The Holly Blood Donor Appeal is just one of these and all addresses are provided in the appendix on page 153.

─────────────── DID YOU KNOW? ───────────────

Who was the puppy's Pa?

Disputed parentage does not only occur in human circles. Lines of inheritance in dogs are important to breed purists and the sire and dam of every puppy has to be given to the Kennel Club (or ruling pedigree dog authority for the country) before a full certificate of pedigree can be obtained.

Sometimes a bitch is mated by two different dogs, during the short season when she will stand for a dog. Usually one dog carefully planned by her owner, and another suitor of her own choice – or who got in by mistake.

There is now a DNA or 'genetic fingerprinting' service available to validate or refute parentage in such cases. (See appendix, p. 157.)

4.   *Peke performance*

Clare Sheldon and her daughter Julie had been living in their new flat only a couple of weeks, when they both returned from work that fateful winter evening in 1980.

As usual, Dougal their Pekingese gave them both an ecstatic welcome, running from one to the other, insisting on a fuss and a pat.

Although there was snow on the ground, Clare immediately set off to give Dougal some exercise, while Julie started to get the evening meal ready.

They were gone less than half an hour, but when Clare returned she was shocked to find Julie lying unconscious on the kitchen floor. She could not rouse her nor find any immediate reason for Julie's deep faint. Very soon she began to feel light-headed herself, and she also passed out.

The next thing she remembers is the frantic pawing of Dougal at her face and the sound of his impatient little cries. She remembers wondering what it was and where she was. Her head was actually moving a little from the dog's determined pawing and his insistence had aroused her, after what was probably only a few minutes.

She felt dreadful, but she crawled to the door and opened it. Slowly she stood up and also opened the window, regaining her strength. Julie still lay deeply unconscious on the floor.

With no telephone yet installed in the new flat, she went outside again and made a number of vain attempts to stop passing motorists. She still felt so unsteady that motorists may have thought wrongly that she was drunk as, to her horror, without exception, they ignored her.

In desperation now, she ran to the nearest house, where a kindly man telephoned for an ambulance, so that Clare could return to Julie.

Still Julie had not moved and her face was deathly pale. Dougal was by now gently licking her face to revive her also, but without

7. *Mrs Clare Sheldon and daughter Julie, who owe their lives to Dougal, the small Pekingese. Dougal received the PRO Dog of the Year gold medal for life saving in 1980.*

avail. There was none of the frantic scrabbling and it was almost as if he knew he did not have the power to arouse her, Clare thought fearfully.

The ambulance came quickly and administered oxygen to Julie, taking her and Clare to the nearby East Riding General Hospital.

The brave little dog was momentarily forgotten in the rush to get Julie to hospital and Clare did not think of him again until Julie was safe and getting the attention she needed.

Then, suddenly, she remembered.

'Poor Dougal,' she said and immediately telephoned a friend, who rushed over to confirm the dog was safe.

Julie was kept in hospital overnight, but allowed home next day.

Investigations afterwards showed that a flue in the kitchen was blocked, preventing the escape of poisonous carbon monoxide fumes, which built up to a lethal level. It was estimated that if treatment for Julie had been delayed another ten minutes, it is unlikely she would have recovered.

And of course, if the dog had not managed to rouse Clare quickly, there would have been no means of getting the ambulance there soon enough.

But how was it that Dougal had escaped the fumes?

The answer is that the build up of carbon monoxide was much lower at ground level because the fumes rise. Clare had been roused because she had not taken in such a large quantity of the posion, but without the dog to disturb her it is unlikley that she would have come round again.

So the small Peke was responsible for saving two lives, and received the PRO Dog of the Year Gold Medal award for life saving in London in December 1980.

Mrs Clare Sheldon said, 'I am very close to my dog. He knows when I am upset or if something is wrong and always nuzzles up to me. But I have always insisted that he does not lick my face. Thank goodness he disobeyed me this time.

'My daughter kept saying in hospital that I had saved her life, but I told her that it was Dougal who had saved both our lives.'

Afterwards an official from East Riding Hospital said: 'Carbon monoxide gas builds up in the blood stream until it reaches a lethal dose. It is known as the 'doze and die' gas. We are sure that a terrible tragedy could have occurred if the dog had not come to the rescue so that these two women were removed from the flat at that time.'

DID YOU KNOW?

How old is your dog?

A rough and ready way to calculate the age of a dog in human terms is to multiply each year of the dog's life by seven. Thus a ten year old dog would be seventy in human terms and a fifteen year old dog would be 105.

But Dr Lebeau, a French veterinarian, has worked out what he believes is a better method. He says that the first year of a dog's life is equal to about fifteen human years, and the second year about nine more. Each subsequent year of a dog's life is equal to another four human years.

According to this method a ten year old dog is about fifty six years of age in human terms and a fifteen year old would be seventy six.

As a general rule, smaller dogs live longer lives than large ones. A ten year old St Bernard is already a very old dog, whereas a fifteen year old small terrier may go on for several more years.

An even more realistic calculation can perhaps be arrived at from the following table, based on Dr Lebeau's calculation for the first nine years of the dog's life, but adding five (rather than four) human years for every year after that.

DOG YEARS	=	HUMAN YEARS
1		15
2		24
3		28
6		40
9		52
12		67
15		82
18		97

5. *Seadogs and water rescue*

Of all water rescue dogs, Newfoundlands are by far the best equipped for life-saving, with their heavy water-resistant coats and feet webbed rather like a duck. Thanks to the courtesy of the Marquess of Hertford, who has a soft spot for these dogs, water trials and tests of endurance designed to keep up to standard the natural ability of the breed are held regularly by the Newfoundland Club of Britain at Ragley Hall in Warwickshire.

These dogs are so robust that they can tow a rowing boat in by a rope held in the mouth and can withstand the cold waters where the breed originated, in Canada. They can readily pull a dog cart as well as rescue people from water. Of all dogs, they are the strongest and most reliable for water rescue, with their natural affinity to water.

Yet when a Newfoundland breed enthusiast was asked recently on a television programme whether, if struggling for his life in the water, he would rather sight a friendly Newfoundland, or a rescue boat, coming to his aid – he had to admit he would opt for the boat every time!

So what chance for a seventeen year old youth, desperately struggling in the river Thames, with only a ten year old arthritic labrador dog between him and the dangerous tidal currents, threatening to suck him under?

This dramatic incident started one day in 1979 when Gary Dodd went for a swim in the Thames at Egham, Surrey. Gary was unaware of the treacherous corkscrew currents in that part of the river and found himself in difficulties while trying to reach mooring posts some twenty yards away. Four times he was sucked under the water, each time with growing terror and panic.

His friend Darren Connor was in the water with him and immediately went to his aid, managing for a time to bravely help keep him afloat. But soon he was in similar difficulties himself.

At this moment, pensioner Osmond Sambrook was walking

8. *Two heroes! Mr Osmund Sambrook received a certificate from the Royal Humane Society and Sandy the labrador retriever won the PRO Dog of the Year gold medal for life saving in 1979. They saved two youths, Gary Dodd and Darren Connor who were in danger of drowning in corkscrew currents in the Thames at Egham, Surrey.*

along the river bank with his ten year old pet labrador retriever Sandy. As he approached them he heard their cries for help.

Without hesitation, Mr Sambrook dived in, fully clothed, to assist the now desperate Gary. After a brave struggle, the elderly man managed to drag Gary to safety.

In the meantime, exhaustion had overtaken Darren.

It was at this point that Sandy joined in the rescue. He jumped into the river and swam over to Darren who was by this time thrashing about wildly. Having reached the youth, the dog appeared to circle, almost as if inviting Darren to hold on to him. Darren put a heavy arm round the dog's neck and struck out as best he could with the other. The strength of the two together enabled them to reach the bank safely and overcome the currents.

Alan Dodd, who is Garry's twin brother, was an eye witness to this event which he described as truly amazing. Alan had himself already tried in vain to reach the swimmers. He said: 'The currents are so strong, I just kept going under when I tried to help in the rescue. Without Mr Sambrook and Sandy there would have been a terrible tragedy'.

The modest Mr Sambrook played down his own part in the rescue but said of Sandy: 'It was his retriever instincts coming out. Sandy is enormously strong and an extraordinary dog. Darren would certainly have drowned without his help. At the time, I was too busy trying to get Gary out of the water to notice what Sandy was doing. I am astonished at this action because he always stays very close by my side. But on this occasion his instinct to help must have been aroused by poor Darren's cries and he swam out about forty feet into the river to help'.

Osmond Sambrook received a certificate from the Royal Humane Society, and Sandy received the 1979 PRO Dog of the Year gold medal award for life-saving in London the following December.

Readers may recall more recent evidence of the way in which death can occur all too swiftly in the dread fast-running currents of the Thames. In the early hours of 27 August 1989, the pleasure cruiser Marchioness was in collison with another vessel, and sank within minutes. Many of the young people aboard who were thrown into the water failed to survive the fast running current and a total of fifty-one people were drowned.

Is there perhaps room for future consideration of a stand-by team of Seadogs for emergency water rescue? Equipped with inflating life-belts round their necks, they would be as welcome as the famous St Bernards sent on mountain rescue missions with their brandy barrels.

Newfoundlands are most often black in colour, sometimes brown, which would make them difficult to see on night missions. But Landseers are a slightly less massive type of Newfoundland, said to have descended from the Pyrenean mountain dog (called Great Pyrenees in America). Base colour of the Landseer is white with black markings. The head is black with a white streak on the muzzle, so it would show up much better in the water.

With the ever increasing role being played by dogs in society today, Seadogs may be just around the corner.

DID YOU KNOW?

President's water-sport

Most dogs like water and all can swim, if they have to. But few can take their water sport quite like Millie the English springer spaniel belonging to President George Bush.

It is reported by the President himself that every day Millie shares a shower with him. No doubt this ensures that both present an equally clean front on every occasion, as well as enhancing the President's reputation as a happy animal-friendly man.

6. *Blinded for bravery*

Sometimes you can get insight into what people expect of their dogs by the names they chose to call them.

Major Stafford Somerfield, well known in dog circles and a past editor of the *News of the World*, politely calls his boxer Mr Smith. I have also known a pomeranian called Miss Prim and a large wolf-hound called Mrs Lewis.

Owners of brave Staffordshire bull terriers have been known to opt for Spartan Warlord or He-Man Himself. Maybe these two are known less formally at home as Spike or Butch. But the names of many show winning dogs leave you in no doubt about the ambitions of the owner. I Have A Dream, My Ambition, Vote for Me, followed by Yet Another Try, all leave little to the imagination. Cruft's supreme champion – look out!

But what of a German shepherd bitch called Sammy? Had the owners hoped for a male dog and then been left with the last bitch in the litter? Or did they decide after the name had been established that Samantha was hardly suitable for a really get-up-and-go type?

However she came by her name, and I never did find out, Sammy features in the next dog drama.

Bernadette Barton who owns Sammy comes from an animal loving family. They have five dogs, a lame mare and a pet lamb, rescued from a bog.

One summer day in 1988 when Bernadette was out walking all her dogs in Smallfield, Surrey, England, a stallion which had been turned out by gypsies suddenly raced towards them.

Bernadette froze with horror as she saw the frenzied horse with a wild look in his eyes start racing towards her. She commanded all the dogs, which are obedience trained, back to the car for safety.

But Sammy, normally the most biddable and obedient of dogs, refused to go back. She placed herself in front of Bernadette and close to the horse as it reared up before them. It was clearly a protective action by the dog who sensed Bernadette's danger. Knowing horses well, exercising with them daily with her horse-riding owner, Sammy knew well enough that this horse was behaving abnormally and that her beloved owner was in danger.

As the horse crashed down on the head of the dog, Sammy screamed in pain and collapsed on the ground. The colour drained from Bernadette's face at the sound of the dog's cries, but she was safe and the horse trotted off as if his mission had been satisfactorily accomplished.

Somehow Bernadette managed to get Sammy back to the car, where the other dogs were waiting patiently. She drove straight to vet David Warnes who gave the dog priority treatment to ease the pain and then set about a series of examinations to assess the extent of the serious head injuries.

The worst damage suffered was to the right eye, where the hoof of the horse had struck directly, and the vet worked to reduce the damage as far as he could so that the dog could go home later that day.

In addition to months of intermittent pain and suffering, the cost of gallantry to Sammy was eventually loss of her right eye. Despite the veterinary care and a second veterinary opinion to try to save the eye, it was causing so much pain to the dog that finally it was decided the only way to stop the pain was to remove the badly damaged eye.

An experience like this can ruin the temperament of a dog for life. But not Sammy. This brave dog was game enough to continue her obedience work, as well as enter skilled agility competitions, in spite of the disadvantage caused by loss of vision and disturbed balance.

Sammy had always had a good extrovert character, willing to do anything her owner asked. Riding pick-a-back style on Bernadette's back has always been good for a laugh and even after her terrifying experience she is willing to enjoy a ride on the back of Berndette's horse.

Sammy knows a good horse when she sees one. And Bernadette knows a good dog.

It would not have been possible to celebrate and publicly reward this, and many more brave dogs, if it had not been for the trouble taken to draw it to the attention of PRO Dogs. It would be encouraging if even more people would follow the bold slogan on the charity's envelopes:

9. Sammy the German shepherd dog lost an eye defending her owner, Bernadette Barton, from a rogue horse, but the dog still takes part in obedience and agility events. Seen here capturing an audience by taking a ride on Bernadette's back.

DOES YOUR DOG DESERVE A MEDAL?
TELL PRO-DOGS!

In the case of Sammy, Mr David Galvin from Bedforshire, who is a member of PRO Dogs, wrote:

'While competing at Newbury and District dog training club open show on 12 June 1988 with my own dog Wookie, I met a young lady with a German Shepherd called Sammy.

'Sammy is a lovely looking dog with a superb temperament and is obviously attached to his owner Miss Bernadette Barton.

'While chatting to Bernadette, I noticed Sammy had lost an eye. I asked how it had been lost and she told me his touching story.

'I feel it would be a fitting tribute to a very brave dog as well as a comfort to Bernadette to have her dog rewarded by one of the 'Oscar' medals and so I am writing to nominate this dog.'

Mr Galvin had not cottoned-on to the fact that Sammy is a female dog to start with, either! Which is where we came in. But this did not matter. All the facts are carefully checked and sifted at the research stage. All that is needed is a nomination and an address or two to start the path which may well lead to a medal.

Sammy received the 1988 medal for devotion to duty with the citation: For bravery in protecting her owner from a rogue horse. And David Galvin was there to cheer the presentation and enjoy the celebration dinner.

Bernadette spoke most articulately of Sammy's rescue when she was interviewed in front of a large audience by presenter Alan Watson. Then she choked back the tears as the gold medal was placed round Sammy's neck.

DID YOU KNOW?
New Breeds into Britain

Every year someone somewhere sees a new kind of dog and decides they have just got to import one or two to start a new fashion.

In the working group* of dogs alone, more than twenty five new breeds have been added since World War Two.

In 1989, the Kennel Club of the U.K. attempted to control this rush of popularity by introducing a new register onto which all previously unrecognised breeds go as soon as the first dog leaves quarantine after the obligatory six month period.

These dogs cannot be shown at Crufts, the best shop-window for British dogs, until such time as there is proof of widespread interest in the breed and that there is a sufficiently large gene pool available for healthy breeding purposes.

Examples of breeds in this restricted register in 1989 include the Shiba Inu from Japan, the Polish Lowland Sheepdog, the Bolognese, the Norwegian Lundehunde and the Grand Bleu de Gascogne.

Note: *the working groups of dogs includes Alaskan Malamutes, Alsatians (otherwise German shepherd dogs), Anatolian shepherd dogs, Australian cattle dogs, Bearded collies, Belgian shepherd dogs, Bernese mountain dogs, Border collies, Boxers, Bouvier des Flandres, Briards, Bullmastiffs, Collies, Dobermanns, Eskimo dogs, Estrela mountain dogs, Giant schnauzers, Great Danes, Hungarian pulis, Komondors, Lancashire heelers, Maramma sheepdogs, Mastiffs, Newfoundlands, Norwegian buhunds, Old English sheepdogs, Pyrenean mountain dogs, Rottweilers, St Bernards, Samoyeds, Shetland sheepdogs, Siberian huskies, Swedish vallhunds, Welsh corgis.

7. Saved from assassination

One of the most exciting medal nominations ever, was for a German Shepherd called Pasha, trained not only as an extremely efficient guard dog but also to disarm anyone holding a gun.

Living in Scotland, country of the brave and the free, in 1988, it is difficult to imagine that all these attributes in Pasha would ever be called to the test. But they were, and at 8 a.m. on 20 October Pasha saved his master, fifty one year old Nikola Stedul, from a would-be assassin.

Mr Stedul was the victim of a carefully rehearsed sensational James Bond type murder attempt, cold-bloodedly planned on that October day. As a black Metro car with the gunman approached, Nikola Stedul was walking with the dog on the outside of the pavement, between himself and the car.

As the gunman took aim, Pasha barked furiously causing distraction and preventing him from firing more accurate lethal shots. Despite the hail of bullets, hushed by the silencer on the gun, which tore into the flesh of Nikola before the vehicle screamed away, Nikola miraculously survived and Pasha was unhurt.

Nevertheless Nikola was seriously injured by the total of six bullets all of which had entered his body, and Pasha stood his ground, guarding his master.

The police and ambulance were fortunately alerted immediately by neighbour Kathy McVicar from her home in Kirkcaldy. Two of the bullets had passed right through Mr Stedul and then through two different windows in their house. One broke a mirror, drawing immediate attention to the sound of breaking glass. Otherwise Mrs McVicar might not have been alerted so quickly.

Nikola's wife Shirley was soon on the scene, waiting in shock as the ambulance arrived. 'I shall never forget being puzzled as the men arrived,' she said. 'First they bent over Nikola, and then they stood up for a moment and seemed to hesitate. I didn't realise until afterwards that it was because they could feel no pulse and feared they were too late'.

Immediate actions to resuscitate Mr Stedul were taken and the doctors were waiting for his arrival at Kirkcaldy hospital some two miles away. He was given a blood transfusion and operated on to remove a bullet critically lodged between his heart and spine as soon as his condition had stabilised sufficiently. This bullet had narrowly missed his aorta and a second bullet had gone through his mouth and out of his neck, just missing his carotid artery.

As his wife Shirley said, 'It was a miracle that he lived. It was meant to be, but there were so many good things working together to save him. If I had written them in a book of fiction, everyone would have said it was too far fetched!'

During the following three week enforced stay in hospital he made a gradual recovery, guarded all the time by the police, lest a further attack be made. Nikola was so anxious to see his faithful dog again that one day the nurses allowed Pasha to be smuggled into the ward for a visit. No doubt this was as beneficial to his health as the many visits by P.A.T. dogs which take place regularly throughout Britain on many hospital wards, where dogs bring a welcome break in routine and a great deal of pleasure to patients.

The background to Pasha's story is a political one involving the strict communist regime in Yugoslavia, and the long term animosity there between Serbs and Croats. The actions of their dreaded secret state security police to bring various Croation exile movements under their control is believed to have led to more than sixty assassinations by the Yugoslav death squad in many different countries. According to Hans Rullmann a well respected West German journalist as reported in the *Scottish Daily Record*, this activity goes back to 1969 and stretches from Canada and the United States to Argentina, across Europe to South Africa and Australia.

Mr Stedul was the president of one of these movements, determined for the oppressed to be free. It is an old familiar theme and one which does not much concern us in a book about dogs.

However it is pertinent to note that the alertness of postal worker Eric Martin, a neighbour who noted down the registration number of the mini Metro the day before the assassination attempt when he thought the driver was behaving suspiciously following a spate of burglaries in the area, was rewarded by the police in a presentation made a year later.

It was this action, followed by the reporting of the number to the police within forty minutes of the incident, that enabled the police to trace the car to Edinburgh airport. Just over two hours later, Vinko Sindicic was arrested aboard an Edinburgh to London plane and charged with the offence.

It was only through this vital swift information that detectives were on the trail in time. Half an hour later, and Sindicic could have made his connection from London and been on the next flight to Yugoslavia, and beyond reach.

On 4 May 1989 Sindicic was brought to trial at the High Court in Dunfermline, Scotland, where he was convicted and jailed for fifteen years.

Throughout the six month period leading up to the trial, Nikola Stedul had been advised to stay away from home at a safe address for his own protection. With the verdict clear, he could at last return to his wife Shirley and daughters Monika and Kristina.

As for Pasha, he was overjoyed to have his master back again. Pasha is a Turkish name and a historical title given to dukes with charge over territories. Pasha is glad to be in charge of his territory and his family, complete once more. No doubt they all feel much safer and happier together, after their terrifying ordeal.

Eric Martin deserved his reward from the police for helping their arrest and Pasha certainly deserved his medal for life saving.

DID YOU KNOW?

The Wonderful Nose

Work in 1989 in Hungary shows that dogs have a more keenly developed and precise scenting ability than even dog experts had appreciated.

With the possible exception of identical twins, every person has a unique and distinctive odour. It is possible for a dog to detect the scent of a person from an object he has held in his hand for just thirty seconds. And the scent remains detectable for up to five years, providing the object is sealed soon after it has been in contact with that person and before it has been cross-scented by other odours.

No doubt as a technique is developed, detectives will seal up items which have been handled by a suspected criminal, for a scent identification parade. New potential for detecting crime will open up, with yet another useful role for dogs to play in society.

II
TERRIERS AND MONGRELS

10. *After a night of celebration at a grand dinner and ball, there's nothing a dog likes better than to show off his medal – and have a fuss made of him by his soldier friend, Lance Corporal Arwel Lewis.*

8.   *The dog soldier*

'Never, ever, will I forget one of my biggest mistakes,' writes the famous international judge, Joe Braddon.

The mistake happened as Joe was watching all the dogs arrive for the PRO Dog of the Year dinner and ball in December 1979, when he had generously agreed to give his services to find the most beautiful dog, by judging the final of the year long annual breed competition. Just one of the elements needed to celebrate the best of British dogs.

Watching the informal parade of magnificent dogs as they arrived to take part at the ballroom in London, he saw a solider with a little mongrel dog. 'Well,' said Joe, 'that's one that won't be going, for sure'.

In fact, that mongrel was Rats the little dog who joined the Army and did a five-year posting in Northern Ireland. The intrepid dog soldier, wounded twice on patrol and the inspiration of many soldiers serving in difficult and dangerous conditions in Crossmaglen. And Rats turned out to be the biggest star of the night.

Full of remorse, that celebrated judge wrote in August 1989: 'Alas, that great little hero Rats has died at the age of seventeen years. I, for one, will mourn his passing and trust if we ever meet again that he will forgive my stupid mistake. I shall never forget him and his proud handler, Corporal Arwel Lewis of the 1st Battalion Welsh Guards, as they stood to attention to receive their well deserved honour.'

So what kind of dog is it that can bring a great breed judge to his knees in admiration and homage? A judge who has had many dogs of his own and who has been called upon to judge the most perfect specimens which man can breed in many countries of the world? And just how did a dog come to join the army in the first place?

The fact is that Rats recruited himself and attached himself originally to 42 Commando, Royal Marines, early in 1978, when he first entered official army records.

How he managed to achieve this distinction, to be followed by many more over the next few years, can be put down only to his remarkable character and self-important waddle which so endeared him to the young men possibly missing their own dogs at home.

There was no shortage of stray dogs round the base in Crossmaglen, but Rats was definitely different. At about Corgi size with a terrier coat he was smaller than most, but what he lacked in size he made up for in jauntiness. He would untie bootlaces in double-quick time, if the feet inside them failed to kick the stone, which he neatly planted by them to indicate time for games.

The Marine patrols never induced his friendship in the first place by offers of food, but came to notice him and even hopefully look forward to seeing him when out on their various patrols. Rats eagerly looked forward to these encounters, waiting for them outside for hours in all weathers until, one day, he was permitted to follow them back to base.

Having managed to get himself accepted, a procession of other bigger and stronger dogs attempted to also join the ranks. But Rats would have none of them, and according to one of the Marines, 'Once Rats was in, he never let any other dog come near us'.

It was soon after this, when Rats was unofficially escorting a patrol, that he was seriously wounded by an IRA bomb. In the same incident, one young soldier died and two other men were wounded. No one had time to think of a wounded dog until the soliders had been seen to, but some time later the little dog was discovered by Lance Sergeant Tim Fielding in a bad state with a hole in his side and both ears cut. It was already several days since the bomb blast and Rats must have crawled away to recover. Certainly no one had seen him since the incident, but one of the soldiers remembered that Rats had been with them and recalled that he had heard a dog screaming in pain.

Major Woodrow was sympathetic to the sorry condition of the poor animal. He gave instructions for the dog to receive the army medical treatment he needed, and he was carefully sewn up again. But Rats was in a low state and went off his food completely. If it had not been for the occasional forced feeding by Sergeant Fielding, it is unlikely that the dog would have pulled through.

After that, Rats pretty much became Tim Fielding's dog, following him faithfully on patrols, obediently trotting to heel, dropping down to the ground and waiting until the command came to go forward again. His anticipation was of the kind normally achieved only after long months of intensive obedience training and his intelligence was a constant source of surprise to Tim.

Rats was game for anything and a great booster to the morale of the men, especially when he refused to be left behind one day and followed Sergeant Fielding on to a helicopter. Most dogs would have been put off by the noise, but not Rats, who became so addicted to this unusual form of canine transport that he would regularly jump aboard any of the many regular flights in the Armagh area.

Eventually he became quite notorious for these helicopter ventures and the army seems to have accepted that if the dog arrived unexpectedly, the decent thing to do was settle him down for the night in the Officers' mess, provide him with a meal and send a message promising to return him to base on the first chopper next day.

It was a sad day for Rats when the inevitable change of duty came round and he had to be parted from the men he had come to know and respect. Several men offered to take Rats back to England but were not permitted to do this. So Rats was passed on with little ceremony, but just the hope that life would be made a bit more cheerful for the incoming Battalion facing their unattractive duties in Crossmaglen.

No doubt at all that these changes of personnel were unhappy for a time for the dog and he pined for the men who left each time, refusing food offered to him. But gradually the perkiness would return and Rats would be ready to serve again.

By September 1979, when PRO Dogs received a nomination suggesting that Rats should be considered for an award, the little dog had experienced three changes of battalion, all of which he had served and worked to protect. In addition to the wounds he received in the first bomb blast, he also received minor burns after a large patrol bomb was directed at the Queen's Own Highlanders, when he was on patrol with them. As a result of these wounds, he had pieces of shrapnel in his body which subsequent x-rays taken when he was very ill later revealed.

In spite of this, his courage was an inspiration to all the men and his fame spread to such an extent that he became known as the 'soldiers' friend'. It was reported that the IRA had put out a contract on him because they knew that if anything happened to Rats, morale would drop to an all-time low.

Major Vyvyan Harmsworth, MVO, of the 1st Battalion, Welsh Guards, was the officer responsible when PRO Dogs made the decision to invite Rats to receive the gold medal award for valour at their annual dinner in London on 9 December.

The army had no hesitation in making all necessary arrangements so that Rats could be present with Corporal Arwel Lewis, assigned to accompany him, for the ceremony.

This involved a journey on a scheduled flight from Belfast and careful attention to providing suitable protection for the dog throughout the London visit. The press photocall in the afternoon prior to the event was well attended, and already it was clear that Rats was going to steal the show. He seemed to sense that the clapping was applause for him and barked excitedly, joining in the fun.

As usual, the caring kennel maids from the Dogs Home Battersea had been invited to look after all the dogs taking part, with loan of special benching for show dogs kindly provided by the contractors.

Rows of benches with beautifully groomed show dogs lined the room beside the ballroom. But show benching was not for Rats. He wasn't going to miss a minute of the action and insisted on taking his place at the dining table where he followed the proceedings with the greatest interest and enthusiasm.

It was actually my pleasure to then read the citation: 'Rats: Dog of War: Delta 7/777: For bravery, devotion to duty and the comfort you have provided to the soldiers serving in Crossmaglen, PRO Dogs is pleased to award your Gold Medal'. The soldier and the dog stood proudly to attention on the stage while this was proclaimed and then as the medal on the tartan ribbon was placed round Rat's neck, the applause started and grew to a crescendo. The excitement mounted and Rats barked and bounced up and down in the air with joy, while Corporal Lewis also smiled with delight.

Few who saw the dog that night would have realised that Rats was still suffering as a combined result of his injuries and his determination never to miss any of the action in Crossmaglen. His urge to protect and join in at all costs was now taking its toll.

Shortly before the London dinner, when Rats had again stopped

11. *Rats the dog soldier, twice wounded on active service in Northern Ireland, on parade with the Prince of Wales' Company, 1st Battalion Welsh Guards.*

eating, Major Harmsworth had arranged for the dog to have a full check up from the veterinary officer at the army dog unit at Long Kesh prison camp. The veterinary report was not encouraging. If Rats was to survive and fully recover from his injuries, it was clear that he would have to retire from his hectic army life.

But Rats was not destined to disappear from the army scene quietly and the following April at the Guard's depot at Pirbright Surrey there was a retirement ceremony which is unlikely ever to be forgotten. Indeed, it will surely go down in the annals of army history.

The Prince of Wales' Company, 1st Battalion Welsh Guards, splendidly attired in black bearskins, with kharki tunics worn on this occasion, stood smartly to attention. Wives, friends and relatives waited expectantly around the parade ground as the personal escort of honour approached to pay an affectionate salute to this war hero.

Rats stepped out with his escort to the salute of the assembled troops. As he trotted past the long line of black boots (not today for a moment tempted to untie a couple for devilment on this so-solemn occasion) the press men started to click their cameras. Television news crews were also present, but not a single one of them could recall a ceremony of this kind for such an unusual retiring soldier before.

A final helicopter ride had been planned as a grand send off, and Rats trembled with excitement and delight as he heard the familiar noise and felt the rush of air from the whirring blades as it approached. He rapidly disappeared past the end of the line of black boots, and started to run as fast as his short legs could carry him. Whether it was for the benefit of the cameras or not we shall never know, but he took a perfectly splendid flying leap off the ground

12. *Rats' heroism recognized by the author, who presented him with the PRO Dog of the Year gold medal for devotion to duty in 1979. Seen here with his handler and friend, Lance Corporal Arwel Lewis.*

and into the waiting helicopter. With never so much as a backward glance, he set off to enjoy a very different kind of life in Kent. And all this was neatly recorded for the world news that day.

Although Rats still had a price on his head, he soon settled down in the Kent countryside with his favourite and most respected soldier master, now willing to spoil him at home as a family pet. With this kindly treatment, his heart condition and general health gradually improved. For security reasons, neither the name of this soldier nor the address in Kent which was the new home for Rats have ever been revealed.

Rats was approximately eight years old when he received his honourable discharge in 1980, but the peak of his fame which followed his medal presentation resulted in considerable fan mail. This arrived not only from dog lovers in the United Kingdom, but also from many countries world-wide.

He continued to make the occasional television appearance for a time and the press seemed ever eager to pick up news of the dog and feature his activities, no matter how modest they might be during his period of convalescence. Rats on a south coast beach with sandcastles even made the news in the summer of 1980.

In 1984 there was a further buzz of excitement when news leaked out that Rats had a couple of terrier girl-friends, and had sired a litter by each of them.

By this time, Rats was twelve years of age. How ever you care to calculate dog years (and various alternatives are offered elsewhere in this book) he was at least sixty-four, and possibly eighty-four, years old in human terms. Not a bad age at which still to be capable of keeping the inheritance going.

There were six puppies in all, three in each family. A total of four bitches and two dog puppies, to be exact.

Josh and Jake, the two males, went to live with their old soldier sire, where Rats seems to have exerted some military discipline to keep them in order. Both pups soon towered inches over their father, as they had not inherited the basset or 'cor' influence from Rats. If you would like some explanation of the 'cor' influence, it is just this. The Corgi is a Welsh dog and the name is derived from 'cor' dwarf and 'ci' dog. Although Rats was far from being a pure bred Corgi, he certainly carried the gene capable of producing this short legged characteristic.

Rats continued to lead a fairly quiet family life, much out of the limelight, until quite suddenly the army announced the news of Rats' death on 23 August 1989.

Seems the old boy suffered a heart attack and collapsed in a corn field. His owner for the latter part of his life is reported in the press as saying: 'We rushed him to the vet who gave him treatment, but he did not recover and died in his sleep that night at home. My wife and I and our young children are absolutely devastated and will miss him sorely'.

A spokesman from Buckingham Palace said that the Queen, who had met Rats after one of the Royal Tournaments, was saddened by the news of his death. The dog hero was widely mourned following news reports and a memorial stone now lies in a corner of Kent, under a maple tree, where once Rats enjoyed the peace of the countryside after a life of devotion and loyalty which few can match.

As for his PRO Dog's medal, that is to be retained and displayed by the British War Museum in London.

DID YOU KNOW?

Bad News for Dogs in Northern Ireland

For reasons which are less than clear, laws to control dogs (or more accurately dog owners) are different in Northern Ireland than the rest of the United Kingdom.

The 1983 Northern Ireland Order raised the dog licence fee there to £5 each year, whilst the rest of Britain was moving towards getting rid of the dog licence fee completely. This was actually achieved under the Local Government Act implemented in May 1989. The huge evasion rate by dog owners 'forgetting' to buy a licence had meant that the fee was actually costing more to collect at 37p per licence than the total sum collected. So it was abolished.

But under the Northern Ireland Order, new fixed penalties were introduced and the time for an owner to find and reclaim a lost dog, or one impounded by a dog warden, was reduced from seven days to five. This meant that owners did not always have a weekend period in which to find their dog, which is of course when most people can devote extra time.

Fixed penalties, kennel fees for dogs impounded and new fines mounted up, so that some owners could not afford to pay the costs of reclaiming their dogs. So the dogs paid the price by facing destruction. Some 8,000 dogs were killed as unclaimed or unwanted, many in electrocution cabinets, in the first full year the scheme operated.

To sweeten the pill of strict legislation, dog owners were assured that all this was really for the benefit of dogs and that once the new dog wardens had rounded up the first lot of strays for destruction, the number of dogs destroyed would soon drop.

Not so. In a written answer to a Parliamentary question on 28 June 1989, Mr Peter Viggers, junior minister at the Northern Ireland office, said that 11,888 stray dogs were rounded up in 1988 and 11,907 put down.

Clearly dog registration with tough laws of this kind have been bad news for dogs in Northern Ireland.

9.   *The super-mum*

Maternal instinct is better developed in some animals than others. Without it any species is endangered and it has occasionally been noted that in some very closely inbred animals the mother refuses to have anything to do with her own offspring. Good qualities may be brought out by close breeding, but so are any unhealthy defects which may also be present in a line. So maybe in the case of such abandoned pups, the mother knows best and the pups are not meant to survive.

There is a similar risk of rejection when the vet interferes with the natural order of things by delivering puppies by caesarian section, as a life-saving measure. If this is a primigravid bitch, that is, pregnant for the first time, the mother may simply not recognise these foreign little bundles as her own as she recovers from anaesthetic, and a great deal of patience and coaxing may be needed to encourage her to accept them.

But what of dogs at the other end of the scale, with an extra strongly developed maternal instinct?

One such was Trendsett Christmas Carol, an English setter bred in 1968 and due on Christmas day, explaining the choice of name.

When Carol was about two years of age, her mother had a second unusually large litter of thirteen pups. Too many to rear unaided and yet every puppy such a fine healthy animal that it was clear they would all thrive with a little care to take the excess strain off Sophie, their mother.

There were six dog puppies and seven bitches, so after the first week as they started to grow rapidly they were divided into two groups by sex for convenience. The girls were put in a whelping box in the kitchen while the boys went into a cosy box with lamp in the garage. The intention was for Sophie to feed the two broods in turn, whilst I gave a little supplementary bottle-feeding help to the other group.

13. *The author's English setter, Trendsett Christmas Carol, with 'adopted' puppy. Carol never had puppies of her own, yet her strong maternal instinct resulted in a milk supply to feed orphan puppies in need.*

Carol had never seen a puppy before but was instantly attracted to the lovely warm puppy smell and the contented noises.

Although at first I attempted to discourage her interest, in case Sophie minded, she became more and more attentive and cuddled down in the box with them whenever she got the chance. She then started the useful clean-up chore, so was allowed to stay. Sophie was typical of the tolerant and gentle temperament of the English Setter and made no objection when she found them together. In any case, she was far too busy with her half-litter in the garage by this time.

After forty-eight hours of full-time mothering from Carol, I went into the kitchen to start the bottle feed. To my amazement, it appeared that the pups were suckling. 'Surely she can't have developed a milk supply?' I thought. But I was wrong. She had milk and fed them successfully until they were weaned. it seems that her close proximity to the pups had stimulated a false pregnancy which resulted in a supply of milk to feed her foster pups.

If it had not been for this personal experience, I might well have doubted the surprising claims made in a nomination received about ten years later for consideration of an award for one of the PRO Dog of the Year medals.

The nomination came from Guilsborough Grange wildlife park in Northamptonshire for Kalli a four year old crossbred collie bitch who had played super-mum to an astonishing variety of babies, including lions, leopards, pumas, Arctic foxes and tigers.

The research which followed revealed the claims to be true. The story started in 1976 when Mrs Beatrice Symington, the owner of Guilsborough park, sent her daughter, Countess Strachwitz, on an errand and she returned with the seven week old puppy, instead of the parrot food for which she had been sent. Kalli soon settled into her new home and began taking a great interest in the other animals there. It was not long before her maternal instinct began to grow.

Beatrice Symington has a great interest in animals and was always keen to bring young ones for the public to see at the park. In 1978 she reports that she heard of a lion and lioness with two cubs kept in unhappy conditions in a local zoo. This was just at a time when new legislation for the protection of wild animals was being implemented, as a result of the 1976 Dangerous Wild Animals Act, and those fearing they might be unable to comply with the

14. *Kalli the super-mum who played foster-mother to an astonishing range of wild baby animals. Seen here with a ten-day-old puma cub who was rejected by his own mother. Kalli fed and raised him successfully.*

demands of local authorities before they would grant a licence were getting rid of their animals.

Mrs Symington was told that she could have the cubs for £50 provided she went into the cramped cage with the parent animals to get them. A daunting challenge indeed! However, with commendable courage and confidence, she faced up to the difficult task.

The faithful Kalli was in attendance and was placed outside the cage as a distraction, whilst Mrs Symington slowly opened the cage door and approached the first cub. She says that fortunately the cub made no sound, which would surely have provoked a response in one or both of the parent animals, and she was able to slowly walk backwards with the cub. The procedure was then repeated for the second cub.

It is believed that shortly after these youngsters were taken away safely, both the lion and his mate were killed. Such a tragedy for these great animals to be taken out of their natural habitat, caged and forced to live in restricted conditions and then shot in the face of a man-made law, designed to protect them. This at a time when the numbers of so many wild cats have been seriously reduced, often to satisfy the greed, need or recreational pleasure of people.

The two cubs which had been saved were christened Sebastian and Sabrina. They were about six weeks old when taken to the park, where Kalli took over duty as foster mum, sleeping with them and licking them clean. She was undoubtedly a helpful factor in rearing them over the first difficult weeks when they demanded much care and attention.

15. *Kalli with a six-month-old leopard cub, already larger than she is but still kept in order and mothered by the amazing foster-mum dog from Guilsborough Grange in Northampton.*

A half-blind brown Capuchin monkey was introduced to the park at the same time and indeed it was the monkey which had attracted the visit to where the unhappy lions were kept in the first place. So the little monkey was indirectly responsible for the rescue of the young cubs.

Kalli's introduction to wild cat cubs having been so successful, it was decided to repeat the experiment carefully some months later when Beatrice heard that a female puma cub had been found in Wales, chained to a caravan and in urgent need of surroundings where she could at least run free. This owner was no doubt also caught up in the need to comply with the 1976 Act.

The new cub was some months older than the lion cubs and about the same size as Kalli when she arrived at Guilsborough. She was named Natasha and although the dog must have seeemd a strange mother-substitute, she soon learned to play quite gently with Kalli, pulling her paw punches so as not to damage her new friend.

Over the years, the reputation which Beatrice Symington had for a knack with animals, grew. This was enhanced by Kalli's reputation as a suitable foster mother, and gradually a number of new cubs were introduced to the park. These included an Indian leopard from Whipsnade zoo in Bedfordshire and three tiger cubs from Howletts zoo in Kent. Incidentally, this last zoo, together with Port Lympne zoo park, were founded by John Aspinall who is frequently in the news and willing to go to enormous lengths to satisfy the driving need which many of us have to understand and enjoy animal companions. But few get the chance to talk to lions and chimps and experience a friendly animal response as John Aspinall, Beatrice Symington – and Kalli, have done.

All the cubs taken to Guilsborough had to be hand reared, usually because the natural mother had rejected them. A time consuming business if done by a single-handed keeper. But thanks to Kalli, they were all kept warm, fed and cleaned. Young animals have to be stimulated before they are able to defecate and this is done quite easily and cleanly by the tongue of the mother. The keeper, on the other hand, will need to spend time gently wiping away with moist warm cotton wool and will then probably have lots of towels to wash and dry afterwards. It is this clean-up which makes the foster mother so especially useful.

There was nothing Kalli liked better than mothering, and her whiskers bristled with delight, rather like a rabbit, each time a new little bundle arrived for her to investigate. And although a dog must smell very strange and foreign to a wild cat, the youngsters soon learned to accept the warmth and comfort offered by this loving little dog. Kalli would nose the cubs into her side and within a few days their presence would have stimulated a milk supply.

Two Arctic fox cubs, brought to Kalli when they were only a few days old, completed the compliment of orphan babies looked after by Kalli, before her nomination for an award came to the notice of PRO Dogs.

The judges decided that Kalli most certainly was well qualified to receive the medal for pet of the year, and on 7 December, 1980 the presentation was made to her in the London ballroom.

Following news of this award, Kalli was invited to be filmed for the popular television progamme *Animal Magic* with that most gentle and kindly of animal lovers, Johnny Morris.

Fame did not stop there, and letters of congratulation started to pour in, some of them with supporting donations.

It was therefore decided to start a local Trust with the money to help in the rehoming of unwanted dogs. Dorothy Radford, a PRO Dogs volunteer, was the scheme organiser.

At the age of nine years, Kalli sadly met an untimely death on 14 February 1985.

At feeding time Kalli always did the rounds and indeed she was a few pounds overweight as a result of the extra titbits she managed to pick up as a result. She never missed a visit to the seals promptly at 2.30 p.m. because after their fish feast which they all shared, the seals enjoyed a game of ball as much as Kalli. So, as usual on that fateful day, Kalli trotted along with a tennis ball in her mouth at the ready.

February that year had been bitterly cold and the water in the lake was frozen over several inches deep, with a fresh fall of snow over the top.

The keeper fed the seals and left Kalli playing ball happily as usual.

It was not until the return of Mrs Symington with some shopping at about 5 p.m. that Kalli was missed.

A search revealed that poor Kalli had fallen into the cold water, where the ice had been broken to feed the seals. Her extra weight had probably prevented her from scrambling out to safety.

Where the snow had been swept away, the black body was visible beneath the ice. Mrs Symington and her family were inconsolable at the loss of this wonderful dog.

The effect of the loss of Kalli was so profound that Mrs Symington became depressed and the following year Guilsborough was sold as a going concern to a new owner. But not before a lasting memorial gravestone had been placed in the grounds.

Beatrice Symington told me: 'Somehow I felt I couldn't go on without Kalli. I had lost the confidence I needed with the animals and without that I could not continue. The animals know when you are not full of confidence and in charge of the situation and you are lost without it'.

What a difference a dog makes.

DID YOU KNOW?
When Good Things End

The trouble with forming a deep attachment is the pain it causes when it ends. The life expectancy of a dog is so much shorter than that of a person, that the loss of a dog is likely to be faced several times in the lifetime of a dog lover.

Although it is considered normal to mourn the loss of another person, society is much less kind when it comes to the very natural similar mourning for a companion animal. When the animal is special, either because of its attributes or because it was continually involved in the day to day activities of the owner, the loss of the animal is very difficult to bear. The death of a pet can be a serious emotional upheaval and remarks such as: 'It's only a dog. You can easily get another one,' are insensitive and difficult to forgive in a person who probably finds it impossible to openly admit to feelings of grief.

Fortunately a number of medical papers have been published, notably since 1970, on various aspects of bereavement, and the work of Dr Colin Murray Parkes in particular seems to have led towards a better appreciation of the way in which people can be made ill following the loss of a companion animal.

In 1989 Dr James Harris, a Californian vet who specializes in grief counselling, received the Bustad Companion Animal Veterinarian Award, which is given for outstanding leadership in promoting the human–animal bond. In the same year, the PRO Dogs national charity in Britain started a limited service to provide counselling to help unhappy people come to terms with the loss of a beloved dog.

10.   *Window cleaner's mate*

Sandy was a different type of dog entirely. The sort who will do anything to please her owner, even if she hates it!

Sandy is a long-haired golden shaggy mongrel, with an appealing expression. Her owner is Stephen Hulbert who was a window cleaner back in 1984 when this report is set, and maybe is still, for all I know.

Sandy was devoted to Steve and reluctant ever to be parted from him. This made it difficult when it came to climbing ladders in the Stalybridge area of Manchester, where Steve worked.

Sandy would sit pitifully at the foot of the ladder, sometimes with a leather helpfully at the ready in her mouth, until Steve climbed down again.

Then, one day, when Sandy had had enough of waiting, she took a few hesitant steps up the ladder towards Steve, and then scurried down again to safety.

It is a fact that even very courageous dogs hesitate to cross areas where there are open spaces. Wooden footbridges, where the odd board is missing, for example. And many dogs refuse to go over roadside grids connected to the road drainage system. Incidentally, that is what makes it so difficult to kerb train a dog conveniently close to these good disposal sites, to reduce fouling. Dogs just don't feel safe walking on or near them.

Ladders present a most unnatural obstacle for a dog to climb. Their feet are not designed to give them a safe grip and they feel vulnerable and unhappy when faced with such a challenge.

It is therefore remarkable that with a little encouragement from Steve, Sandy eventually learnt how to climb to the top of even very extended ladders, just to be near Steve.

Steve also taught her how to carry a small bucket in her mouth and fetch and carry cleaning cloths and wash leathers as the need arose.

News soon spread about the cute dog that helped to clean the

16. *Sandy the window-cleaner's mate who leared to climb ladders so as not to be left behind when his owner Stephen Hulbert went window-cleaning.*

windows and people wanted to see for themselves whether Sandy really could climb ladders. It was very good for business.

The local paper took an interest and soon after that, Sandy and Steve received an invitation to be filmed for the popular BBC television programme, *That's Life*. Following this, PRO Dogs received a shoal of nominations suggesting that Sandy should be considered for a medal.

The judges who sit each year to decide from the short list which dogs are to receive the annual medals are all very fond of dogs. In general they will not select a dog which they feel has in any way been exploited or made to do anything which is contrary to the normal instinct of a dog.

Sandy's case was ticklish. However the dog had certainly not been forced to climb ladders. She had made herself overcome natural fear in order to be closer to her owner. Clearly this devotion deserved recognition and the unusual nature of the nomination made Sandy a good candidate for pet of the year.

Sandy was invited to receive the 1984 award with due ceremony in London, much to the delight of her owner. As usual, the press took considerable interest in the canine 'Oscar' awards and insisted that Sandy gave a demonstration of ladder climbing for the papers next day.

A ladder was eventually found, but Sandy was very reluctant to climb. No amount of setting her on the bottom rung, making encouraging noises and offering of titbits worked. It was only when one of the PRO Dogs hostesses politely pointed out that the element needed to make Sandy climb was missing, that the problem was resolved. That element was of course for Sandy to reach Steve.

Success was eventually achieved when Steve climbed the ladder first and Sandy obligingly followed.

After the dinner, a number of people who were delighted by Sandy's antics approached Steve and asked him to train their dogs to climb ladders. The reason why it never worked will be plain to see, when considered from the point of view of the dog.

Clearly the idea of a ladder-climbing dog greatly appealed to public imagination because Sandy was widely photographed and reported. She even appeared as a comic strip on one occasion in the *Beano* comic. In addition, she was picked by Barbara Woodhouse, that most famous of dog trainers, as most lovable mongrel in the North West in a dog show competition.

Sandy's head for heights was also celebrated in quite a different way by the Manchester Skydivers' Club, where an honourary membership was conferred on her for being a 'top' dog. Stephen was himself a member of this parachutists club and as we know – everywhere that Stephen went, that dog was sure to go!

DID YOU KNOW?

No Dogs in Parks?

A wave of intolerance to dogs seemed to cross the North Atlantic ocean from the United States to Britain towards the middle of the 1970's. In New York, dogs were banned widely, restricted to on-leash exercise only and strict laws enforced on dog owners.

PRO Dogs was set up in an endeavour to meet it, and spread knowledge of how dogs can provide benefits for people.

The first total bans on dogs in England were in main parks in Burnley, Lancashire in 1977. They were introduced under powers derived from antiquated local laws, known as the Burnley Borough Improvement Acts.

The battle of Burnley dog owners versus Burnley Borough Council was a saga of some standing. It was taken away from the courts of local jurisdiction and transferred to the High Court in London by the Council in a bid to enforce their action, despite escalating costs which had to be paid for by local ratepayers. Some saw it as an act of intimidation designed to bring to their knees the dog owners, also faced with huge legal costs if they were to defend their position.

It was fought with dogged determination by a British sense of outrage against this infringement of traditional freedom to enjoy a stroll in the park with a dog.

It finally resulted in Mrs Mavis Thornton, a social worker, mother of a number of children, owner of several dogs and one of the group of objectors, being sent to Holloway prison for three weeks for failing to give a High Court Judge an undertaking to obey the controversial new byelaws.

Although the battle was all but lost, an important stand had been taken by a brave few. Had it been more widely recognised as the first in a whole line of new laws to curb dogs from an increasing number of public open spaces and even from beaches, dog owners might well have united more effectively to throw it out.

11. *The partnership*

When the kindly, diminutive Miss Angela Law retired as matron of a home for the elderly, she missed very much all the people she used to see every day in the course of her work.

She lived alone in a flat and if it had not been for Toby, her smooth coated dachshund-related dog, she would have been lonely.

Toby was a busy dog. He went everywhere with Miss Law and he caused her to meet and chat to people in a way which would not have been possible without him.

Toby would discover a discarded coke can and roll it along the ground at an amazing rate, causing anyone about to exclaim to Miss Law about her amusing dog. Or he would grab the corner of a large torn poster in an alleyway, and rush along enjoying the noise it was making. Toby was an ice-breaker and a bit of a show-off. And he gave Miss Law something to gently chide and scold.

One weekend at the end of April 1985, Miss Law was taking Toby for his usual late night walk, when he became agitated near to a gas point in the gardens of a block of flats known as Reynolds House on the South Ham estate on the way back to their flat in Basingstoke. He barked insistently until the windows flew up and neighbours shouted pointed advice in no uncertain terms to Miss Law.

So she dragged him home.

But Toby seemed to know there was something wrong. Something in need of further investigation. And he refused to be quiet. He whined and barked and pawed the door.

Miss Law pondered. It wasn't his usual bark. It certainly wasn't his what-are-we-going-to-do-to-make-her-laugh-today? bark nor even his I'm-not-ready-to-settle-down-for-the-night-yet bark. It was a new noise he was making. More of a if-you-don't-listen-to-me-and-do-something-quickly-we'll-all-die bark thought Miss Law. And fortunately she was enough in tune with Toby to recognise the urgency, put on her coat and investigate further.

Without hesitation, Toby dashed out the moment the door opened and charged back to the gas point. He sniffed round excitedly. By this time Miss Law could smell it too. Gas. A major gas leak. Quickly she returned to the flat and alerted the police and the gas board.

Both responded quickly and in no time had the situation under control. Residents were roused and evacuated in their pyjamas. Where tenants did not respond speedily, doors were forced open to ensure that all the flats were vacated.

17. *Having received the PRO Dog of the Year medal for life-saving, Toby finds his happiness completed with the gift of a dog chewdle bone presented by Katie Boyle.*

Midnight drilling started to establish the source of the leak and continued extensively. As neighbours waited anxiously for the engineers to deal with the emergency, they made each other cups of tea. They also reminded each other ruefully about some of the insults they had hurled at Toby a short time earlier.

Toby was the hero of the hour and the next day the local Basingtoke and North Hants Gazette carried a large front page photograph of Miss Law and Toby with blazing headline 'Dog saves the lives of council tenants'.

A Southern Gasboard spokesman said: 'Toby is a hero. It was a leak which could have had serious consequences'. The experts agreed that it was only thanks to prompt action by the emergency services that an explosion was prevented.

Following this incident, the town's seventy year old cast iron gas mains were ripped up and replaced by polythene pipes.

Mrs Lesley Catchpole, a member of PRO Dogs living in Basingstoke, saw the press news item and sent it in to the head office of the charity with her nomination of Toby for an award.

The nomination was successful and on 1st Decenmber 1985 Toby received a medal for life saving.

Miss Law made the journey to London with her brother and was overcome with delight. She was invited to appear with Selina Scott on *Breakfast Television* next morning and she was promised a portrait of Toby as a lasting memory of her dog, kindly donated by artist Doreen Vincent. She was also featured on the national news. When asked to comment on the occasion, she said:

'Dogs have not had much of a press lately so perhaps this restores the balance a bit. As for the gold medal, I don't know what to say, except that I think it is the most exciting thing that has ever happened to me. And Toby, of course.'

And the sympathetic partnership stepped down together off the stage, Toby carrying the large dog-chewdle bone, thoughtfully given to him by Katie Boyle who was present as guest of honour to support the event.

DID YOU KNOW?

Hambling

Hambling literally means mutilating, and all manner of cruel operations were performed on dogs in the past, either to prevent them from hunting or as a means of keeping them within limited confines.

It was not only perfectly legal for dog owners to cripple their dogs but in medieval times shepherds and herdsmen were required by dictate to mutilate their dogs in various ways to prevent them from taking the game of their titled or royal masters.

Hambling involved cutting off the pads of the dog's feet or making a deep cut crossways on the ball of the foot.

Iris Combe has much of interest to say on the subject of the history of ancient laws in her book on herding dogs.

According to the Oxford English Dictionary on Historical Principles, hambling was mistakenly taken to mean hamstringing in the 17th and 18th centuries and perhaps this was because both hambling and the cutting of the tendon known as the hamstring were used to cripple dogs at this time.

It could be argued that the keeping of dogs today within strict kennel confines and never permitting them the regular free running exercise they need, is as cruel.

12. *Buried alive*

Micky the Jack Russell terrier and Percy the Chihuahua were sworn enemies. It wasn't so much that they disliked each other, but rather that they were in fierce competition for the attention of their owners. This resulted in a few scraps and a lot of interesting involvement for the dogs, as well as amusement for the family. The scraps were never serious.

Micky belonged to Mr Bill Perks, a retired local government officer, and his wife Jean, who lived in Barnsley, Yorkshire. Percy belonged to their married daughter, Christine. The fun and the sparring matches started on Christine's frequent visits to see her parents with her baby son, Alex, and Percy.

On one of these visits, on 21 April 1983, Christine noticed that Percy was missing. The family went outside to look for him and were shocked to see him lying in the road at the front of the house beside a car that had stopped. He had only just been knocked down.

Percy was lying motionless. Blood was oozing from his mouth and from a cut under his chin. Christine said, 'We were all crying and the woman driver of the car was also in tears.'

Gently Percy was carried into the house and laid on the kitchen table. Mr Perks felt his heart, but there was no heartbeat. It seemed that Percy had died at once of his injuries and in view of the heartbroken reaction of Christine and his wife, Mr Perks decided that the kindest thing was to bury poor Percy in the garden right away.

The weather was damp as Mr Perks set out to dig a grave some eighteen inches deep for Percy, at about noon that day. Percy was laid in a strong paper sack and buried with due grief and Christine returned sadly to her own home, with her mother.

Several hours later while Mr Perks was sitting watching television, Micky came into the room with filthy muddy paws, and started whining and crying. He was restless and unhappy and he

18. *Happy Mrs Christine Harrison with her Chihuahua Percy who was brought back from the dead after being buried alive – thanks to the vigilance and persistence of Micky the terrier.*

tried to paw at Mr Perk's trouser legs. 'I realised afterwards that he was trying to tell me something,' said Mr Perks, 'but at the time I told him to go away, and thought nothing of it'.

It was clear that the dog was anxious to go outside again, but Mr Perks did not want any more mud brought into the house so he kept him in.

Then at about 7.30 p.m. some seven hours after Percy had been buried, Mrs Perks returned from her visit to Christine and went into the house by the back door. She glanced down the garden and to her horror saw the body of Percy lying on the garden path. She went in to report the gruesome find to her husband.

For a short time, Micky was in disgrace. Mr Perks was ready to give Micky a good hiding for digging up Percy's body.

He was scolding Micky as he let him out to go and re-bury Percy. But Micky was interested only in returning to Percy, where he at once started to lick frantically at the face of his old sworn enemy.

Mr Perks was dismayed. And then he got the shock of his life. As he bent down he could see that Percy was breathing and his body was warm, although the dog's eyes were closed. Percy's face was quite clean and it is likely that Micky had been licking Percy's face some hours earlier immediately he had dug up the body, which was probably a critical factor in saving the life of the dog. It is clear that when Micky dug up the body of the Chihuahua his canny instinct had told him the dog was still alive.

It is known that the keen scenting ability of a hunting dog can detect whether an invisible prey is dead or alive and dogs used in mountain and disaster rescue can also detect bodies and indicate by the kind of bark they make whether that person is likely to be alive or dead. Micky's own natural terrier instincts would have been alerted, as used in negative pursuits such as badger baiting, and he followed this urge to dig, with lifesaving results.

Mr Perks hurried to deal with the situation which now showed itself in such a different light. 'Good boy, Micky,' he said, and then shouted to his wife to bring a towel to wrap up Percy warmly.

At once they telephoned Christine to give her the news and Glenn, Christine's husband, drove round to collect Percy and rush him to the Abbey veterinary clinic in Barnsley.

For four days Percy hovered between life and death. Christine said, 'I went to see him every day, but they said there wasn't a lot of hope for him. He was alive, but seemed to be in a sort of coma. They thought there might have been some brain damage and we even talked about having him put down. I couldn't stand the thought of him being just some kind of vegetable'.

Then on the morning of the fifth day, Mrs Turner, an assistant at the veterinary clinic, went in and found Percy standing up and wagging his tail. 'As soon as they phoned me, I rushed down to the vet's,' said Christine. 'I could hardly believe it. He was still weak on his feet but he had made a full recovery and after spending another day at the vet's we were able to bring him home'.

Percy was soon back to his old self, but he didn't seem a bit grateful to Micky. They continued as the best of enemies, jealous of each other and snapping as soon as one dog felt the other was getting too much affection from Christine.

Although no one knows exactly how long Percy was buried, it must have been for at least two hours. It may be that the air trapped in the paper sack kept Percy alive for long enough, before Micky got to work. Certainly Micky was standing by when Mr Perks buried Percy.

The magazine *Titbits* nominated eight year old Micky for one of PRO Dog's gold medal awards in May and the judges agreed when they met in September that Micky should receive the 1983 award as Pet of the Year.

Following this, Micky built up quite a fan club. A breeder of Jack Russell terriers, admiring the fine instincts of the dog, asked to pay for his services at stud and a dog lover who read about the report in Northern Ireland sent some money to buy him some meat.

Local children often called into the house asking to see Micky and bringing him food and the vet who treated Percy, Mrs Teresa Westmorland, said it was a most remarkable story.

'I've never heard of anything like it before,' she said, 'and Micky certainly deserves the official award. It is remarkable that a dog could rescue another dog in this way and that Percy could have survived underground. After he was brought in it was touch and go if he would make it, but somehow he pulled through. We are all delighted.'

This is certainly a story which deserves a twist in the 'tail'. Perhaps this can best be achieved by shaking up an old phrase:

With enemies like Micky, who needs friends?

───────────── DID YOU KNOW? ─────────────

Dogs Help Postmen

Teams of sniffer dogs are used to make the job of postmen safer.

By the end of the 1980's a team of eight dogs was used at the port of Dover alone, to check that incoming mail contained no explosives or drugs.

Each of these trained dogs intercepts an average of ten dangerous hauls each year, often with a street value runing into thousands of pounds.

Dogs used are mostly gun dogs, with Labradors and English Springer Spaniels as favourites. These dogs have highly developed scenting ability and are trained by Royal Airforce dog handlers for their specialized work.

Dogs are usually donated by members of the public, often when they discover they have a dog which needs a lifestyle more active than they can provide at home. The dogs are retired at about eight years of age and are then either returned to the donating home or bought out by their trainers, who usually grow very fond of them.

The buy-out fee is set at a low level intended to be no obstacle to a happy life of retirement with a handler who cares. 1989 price was £10 plus vat (value added tax presently set at 15%).

13. North and South Pole dog

No expedition is complete without a mascot and this was to be the fate of a small Jack Russell puppy, taken away from his mother at just four weeks of age and given to those intrepid explorers, Sir Ranulph and Virginia Lady Fiennes.

The puppy was christened Bothie, and he was two years of age by the time the plans for the transglobe expedition were complete and commercial sponsorship obtained to pay for every single item of expenditure. Even Bothie's dog food was to be paid for, as well as the expensive obligatory six months period behind bars in quarantine kennels, which the dog would have to face on return to Britain.

Dogs most willingly accompany their owners wherever they go and whatever deprivations they have to accept. To be with their owners is all that they ask.

Bothie's initial shock was to be parted first from Ranulph and then, just a few days later, from Ginnie, when they both set out ahead to complete the first stages of the journey by ship from London to Cape Town. Bothie had three months to wait until it was time for him to fly out to join the party with a supply of additional cargo.

In December 1979, Bothie was protestingly shut into a small regulation size animal carrying box and deposited in a Boeing 727. Travelling alone by air in the cargo hold of an aircraft can be a terrifying experience and some dogs accept it better than others. Even on landing, the ordeal was not yet over. A further long hot journey by road would have been avoided if the plane had landed at Cape Town. However British Airways who paid for all the expedition cargo flights stopped only at Johannesburg. The two day onward journey in a car like an oven was the first experience in temperature extremes which the little dog had to face.

The reunion which eventually followed was joyful and Bothie was given the welcome he deserved. His cheeky and perky character was the best morale booster the expedition team could have had to keep

19. *Sir Ranulph Fiennes with terrier Bothie on the 1980–82 transglobe expedition to the North and South Poles.*

them going in their self imposed dangerous and difficult journey.

It was just as well that Bothie lost no time in making firm friends with the ship's cooks and ensured himself some extra food, because soon after leaving Cape Town the ship met fearsome storm conditions. Poor Bothie groaned pitifully as the wind lashed the sea and the ship rolled and vibrated with alarming sounds. Dogs suffer seasickness, too.

The problem of where to go – when a dog's got to go, was never resolved and Bothie found himself in disgrace with each member of the crew in turn when he visited their cabin and left the unmistakable evidence that he had paid a call.

But the happy times came too and Ginnie spent hours playing endless games of ball, or hunt-the-squeaky-frog. Bothie loves to stand on the boat deck, watching the sea below when it was calmer, but he had to wear a harness attached to a lead to ensure that he was not washed overboard.

He guarded the ship territorially, seeing off any sea birds which might dare perch on the rails and lifting his leg on the outer boundaries to scent mark in the time honoured way.

Early in the New Year of 1980 the ice cliffs of Antarctica were spotted and Bothie was soon on the strangest icy land he had ever seen. Penguins and seals nearby brought him new exciting animal scents as he sniffed the air in the light breeze. At least it was firm land at last, even if it was to prove most inhospitable.

Bothie was the first terrier to set foot on the largest coldest continent in the world. He shivered, and Ginnie wrapped him up in the smart polar gear of warm coat and ear covers to protect him from the biting cold.

Bothie was soon to grow his own extra thick coat and his diet, in common with all the members of the expedition, contained extra fats to help keep out the cold.

Eight long months including the Antarctic winter were spent with four members of the team in a cardboard hut at the base camp. During this time Ranulph and the rest of the team set off for their trek across the Antarctic through the South Pole.

Day and night were permanently dark, so that the days seemed interminably long. It was then that Bothie's antics gave vital

20. *A delighted Bothie, reunited with his owners, Sir Ranulph and Lady Fiennes after the terrier's stay in quarantine for six months, when they returned to Britain in 1982.*

moments of light relief and he was more than a mascot. He was the reason to stay sane. To laugh and have fun.

The front team reached the South Pole in laborious stages on their skidoo sledges and achieved their destination on 15 December 1980. Bothie with the back up team completed the journey more easily by air, in seven hours, landing at the South Pole strip to celebrate Christmas together. The Americans at the permanent base there made a great fuss of Bothie and gave them all a Christmas to remember.

Huskie dogs pulling sledges cause no surprise in arctic circles, but no one had ever taken a Jack Russell terrier to the South Pole before.

Bothie had conquered the South Pole, but he was still to suffer the journey to the North Pole. Further extremes of temperature lay ahead. The heat in crossing the equator and the sub zero temperatures of the distant ice cap. At least the journey by ship allowed the opportunity to become acclimatized to the changes.

The worst blow for Bothie may well have been when yearning for some lovely green grass to run on, he was not permitted to go ashore when the ship stopped first at Campbell Island, an uninhabited nature reserve, and then in New Zealand. He had to watch while they all went ashore without him.

At every port, more free supplies of food and other commodities were begged and those willing to provide them came aboard with their offerings. This gave Bothie a chance to make many new friends and sometimes children would return again and again to see him.

The Jack Russell club in Australia sent special messages of cheer to Bothie but in Sydney, once again, he was refused permission to go ashore.

As the ship sailed off once more towards Suva the heat became unbearable for one small dog who had grown a bear-like coat to protect him from arctic conditions. Day after day he lay collapsed and panting on the coldest floor he could find.

On one occasion he managed to cool off by swimming with members of the crew in the shark-infested waters of the Pacific ocean. There can be few canines who have experienced as many undoglike adventures as Bothie, although other possible contenders could be Laika, the first living creature to travel in space and Belka and Strelka, the first dogs to return alive from space travel. However, none of these poor dogs enjoyed the companionship of their owners to share their terrifying adventures and it is the man-and-dog-together element which makes experience bearable and enjoyable for the dog.

The coastline of the United States promised freedom to run on dry land for Bothie at last and there would be many more opportunities as he travelled with Ginnie in a Land Rover up through the bear country of British Columbia and onward through the Yukon and the North West territories.

Mosquitoes in large numbers were a problem and Bothie was driven wild with the irritation. Stops were made at various motels and Bothie enjoyed swimming in Ginnie's bath water which appeared to give some relief from the irritating bites.

Life at the Tuktoyaktuk base held a great deal of interest for Bothie, which turned out to be inhabited by gophers. These little ground-squirrels provided many hours of happy but frustrating sport and exercise. The gophers worked as a team in an effort to outmanoeuvre Bothie, disappearing down a hole to safety just when they were tantilisingly almost within his grasp.

But it was a litter of black puppies out of a Newfoundland bitch and thought to be by a husky × Labrador dog which gave him the canine companionship he needed.

Ginnie can hardly have been looking for another dog to complicate the final stages of the expedition, but she may well have had in mind the long quarantine period which Bothie would face on return to Britain in 1982, as she watched the friendship develop between Bothie and the one black puppy finally left from the litter.

The black puppy grew and grew. And so did Bothie's affection for her. They were inseparable. It would have taken a harder heart than Ginnie's to leave behind the large affectionate puppy when they set off to join the advance party for the final stage to the North Pole.

Despite obstacles and difficulties (which included the loss of equipment in a fire and newspaper headlines proclaiming 'Polar expedition in flames' and 'Team cut off in race to Pole') on Easter Sunday 1982 Ranulph and his team finally made it. A film crew touched down on the only flat strip near the Pole to record the occasion, and Bothie was there to be in on the act.

This was Bothie's moment of glory. This was the triumph he had suffered to achieve. Bothie – the only dog to have lifted his leg on both the North and the South Pole.

Others may have noticed that Ranulph, Ginnie and team achieved it, too. But this is a dog book.

21. *Bothie dances with joy at the PRO Dog of the Year awards dinner in London, December 1982, when he received the gold medal for pet of the year.*

That year, PRO Dogs received many nominations and the judges agreed to award Bothie the gold medal for Pet of the Year. The awards dinner was to be held in November and fortunately Bothie and black dog had completed their six months in quarantine kennels by then.

PRO Dogs also invited Bothie and Ginnie to their charity stand at Crufts the following February. This involved special dispensation from the Kennel Club as usually only dogs which have qualified for Crufts and are entered for competition are permitted at the show.

Sir Dudley Forwood, Chairman of Crufts, not only allowed this but extended the invitation to allow Bothie to make an appearance in the main ring. A rare honour for a breed which, as I write, has only just been recognised by the Kennel Club.

Sir Dudley was always one for a sporting dog, and a bit of a sport, himself.

DID YOU KNOW?

Protecting Your Dog in a Will

There was an outcry when wealthy Nottingham widow, Mrs Diana Busfield, left all the money in her will to charity, with the exception of £20,000. This was left specifically in 1988, when she died, to provide care for her much loved Yorkshire terrier, Benjy.

For six days, Benjy was the richest dog in town, but, pining for his owner and familiar surroundings, he began biting and snapping at staff in the kennels where he had been put. So he was destroyed.

A spokesman for the PRO Dogs charity said, 'I can't help thinking that Mrs Busfield would not be very happy to know that the animal had survived for only six days when she had left so much money for him to be looked after. The dog needed care in a home-like situation by someone who really knows the breed. This could have been arranged.'

The Benjy story, which received attention by the press, is an indication that people who are very concerned about their animals are often not able to make sure that their wishes are carried out.

Andrew Bowden, the Parliamentary spokesman for PRO Dogs, raised questions about protection for animal beneficiaries of a will. It turns out that this is a complex matter. Animals are the property of their owners and therefore cannot themselves be left a bequest or property directly, at least as far as English law is concerned.

There are, however, ways in which a dog can be written into a will and be protected in the event of their owner suffering any sudden emergency or death. Information has now been published as a direct result of Benjy's story. (See bibliography page 152).

14. *Giving more than was asked*

Very many working police dogs have been nominated for one of the PRO Dog of the Year gold medals, but few have succeeded. All police dogs are required to work to a high standard and to win a medal the dog has to do even more than was expected of him in training.

But a police dog did win the medal for devotion to duty in 1981 and again in 1984.

First to win was Dannydeer Franz, a longcoated German Shepherd dog from the Grampian Police Force in Aberdeen, Scotland.

This dog was bred by a family in Aberdeen and donated to the police at the age of five months. He was puppy walked and trained by the Sergeant in charge of the dog section, as is the usual custom, and from a very early age showed great potential in tracking and searching by scent.

In April 1981 Franz was allocated to Constable Allan Hendry and they quickly developed the good understanding of each other which is essential for team work in emergency situations.

By June of that year the twosome was rated as fit for operations and quickly became successful in searches and arrests.

Then on the afternoon of Sunday 21 December Franz and his handler were called by Aboyne, Aberdeenshire, where an eighty-two year old man had been reported missing from a home for elderly people, over three hours earlier.

The temperature was below zero and large expanses of ground were covered with snow and ice. Conditions were far from ideal for tracking. Franz was given an article of clothing from the old man, to sniff, and managed to pick up the missing man's scent from outside the gates of the home. He followed the track for about half a mile but then it petered out due to the difficult weather conditions. The search continued at a farm where it was then confirmed that the man had been seen. Suddenly Franz was on the track again and Allan Hendry let him go free. The dog went over a gate and down a track and soon the policeman heard the dog barking excitedly. As he approached, he also heard the feeble sound of the old man. Soon he could see that the man was lying on the snow covered ground unable to get up after having slipped and fallen.

As quickly as possible the old man was taken back to the home where he was given medical treatment for exposure. The local doctor who attended said the poor condition of the man showed he would soon have died of hypothermia in the cold weather conditions that day, and the police officer said he did not think the old man would have been able to survive another two hours, if the dog had not found him.

Within two weeks, Franz and Constable Hendry were called to the rescue again. This time for a little boy who disappeared from the centre of Aberdeen early in the afternoon of Monday 29 December 1980, while out on a shopping trip with his parents.

When they could find no trace of the boy the parents became very anxious and a massive police search was started.

In answer to appeals on television, a member of the public reported seeing a young child on the Stonehaven road a mile or so south of the city.

At about 7 p.m. that night, Franz and Constable Hendry set out in the direction of the sighting in cold wet and dark weather conditions. Searching in the mud beside the hard shoulder, a police officer found a single, small footprint. From this, Franz picked up the scent of a child and immediate began tracking along the grass verge, despite the difficulty caused by fumes from passing traffic.

The dog worked hard, anxious not to lose the important smell, but stopping occasionally, confused by other distracting scents.

At last, after tracking for over a mile and a half in pitch dark, Franz suddenly started to bark.

'We shone a lamp into some tall grass,' said Allan Hendry, 'and there was the wee boy, frozen, terrified and crying his eyes out'.

German Shepherd dogs, or Alsatians as they used to be called, are often regarded as fierce and fearsome dogs. But within the space of eight days an old man and a young child had good reason to be thankful for one of these wonderfully trained and intelligent dogs.

22. *Courageous police dog Khan continued in action despite severe pain after being run down by a car. Seen here before the presentation of his PRO Dog's canine 'Oscar', with his handler Allen Bratchell in 1984.*

For complete reliability, a bond of understanding has to grow between the handler and the dog which makes the work of such a twosome invaluable, as well as being satisfying to both.

Grampian police were pleased to send Franz to London to receive his medal in 1981, where he must have won over many in doubt about the breed with his gentle and perfect behaviour.

Another policeman and dog team working in harmony were successful in the 1984 nominations.

Dogs of good character are always needed for police work, but even perfectly trained dogs are not expected to continue working immediately after they have suffered severe internal injuries.

The courage of police dog Khan, another German Shepherd, surprised Constable Allen Bratchell, his handler, even though he always had the highest regard for the performance of his dog, who was once an unwanted stray puppy.

In August 1984, Allen Bratchell and Khan answered an emergency call. The dog was sent after two youths suspected of making a hoax telephone call to police in Croydon, South London. This was in connection with an armed robbery in East Croydon.

Said Constable Bratchell, 'Khan went after them, but as he rounded a corner I heard the screech of car brakes'.

The dog had been run down by a car. All the officer could see of him as he arrived on the scene were his legs sticking out from under the car. He was trapped and howling in great pain.

With the superhuman strength which comes to us in an emergency. Allen Bratchell managed to lift the front of the car sufficiently to free the poor dog. And then, to his amazement, the dog took off again after the two suspects.

After a lengthy chase, brave Khan cornered the youths and held them at bay until his master caught up with him. Only then did he collapse to the ground in agony.

The youths were taken to the police station and Khan was admitted as an emergency to veterinary hospital. He had crushed ribs, a punctured lung, internal bleeding and a broken leg. Later he developed a lung embolism and his life was saved only by the skilled care he received during his six week stay in hospital.

The PRO Dogs judges were unanimous that Khan should receive a medal for devotion to duty, but there was concern in case the dog was not fit enough to receive it. The award was due to be presented just four months after Khan was injured so seriously, and it is a condition of the medal presentation that the dog must be there to receive it.

Allen Bratchell, who had two young children at the time, did manage to attend the dinner with Khan. He said: 'The whole family loves Khan. They were upset by the extent of the dog's injuries. But he had recovered in time to receive his medal. He always was a winner!'

The citation was for courage in spite of suffering and injury and the national press covered the award with enthusiasm. Next day large photographs of the handsome police officer and dog appeared on the main pages and as I accompanied the two to the breakfast television studios next morning it seemed I had never seen a happier dog or one which looked at his handler with a more melting and devoted expression.

Here was a dog who had clearly demonstrated that there was nothing he would not do to please his master.

DID YOU KNOW?

Police dog ate evidence

Police dogs are called upon to work in difficult and sometimes dangerous circumstances. Their record is very high and they save a great deal of cost in extra man hours which would be needed without them. Therefore on the rare occasions when something goes wrong, it makes news.

On 25 September 1982, *The Daily Telegraph* reported that members of a jury at Canterbury Crown Court had been told in a robbery case that they could not see the exhibits. This was because the police dog which had found the evidence had also eaten it!

Busby, a German shepherd dog, had been called in to find a bag containing a loaf of bread, some mincemeat and a box of matches which had been thrown into a quarry in Northfleet, Kent. Before Busby's handler could get to the bag the dog had eaten the mincemeat.

Mr Andrew Goymer, prosecuting counsel, told the jury: 'Unfortunately you will not be able to see any of the exhibits because they have all been eaten by the police dog.'

III
THE BEST OF SERVING DOGS

15. *Sheep rescue*

Few people rely more on the assistance of working dogs than farmers and shepherds. Even with the progress of modern technology, the value of these dogs is beyond price.

In her book on herding dogs, Iris Combe traces the origins and development in Britain of many different breeds used as herding or stock dogs, with much interesting detail, but the sensitive and highly intelligent working border collie is undoubtedly the number one choice for shepherding today.

No one has brought the thrills and skills of sheepdog trials to public attention better than Phil Drabble, as presenter of the popular BBC television series entitled *One Man and His Dog*, with his co-presenter Eric Halsall. This programme features dogs fully stretched mentally and active as they ought to be. How many townsmen must have wondered at this country scene brought to their living-room screen, showing dogs at their most loyal and intelligent – at their most cunning and cute – working in perfect harmony with man? And what a great deal it must have done in fostering better understanding of dogs.

Life on the farm is often harsh for dogs, even today, and not all receive proper care to their coats and a just reward for their work. Dogs never complain. And they don't belong to a union.

Many receive due appreciation, and one such was farm dog Nipper, owned by Mr E A Norris, in 1985.

One day in February that year, when lambing was just about complete on Ansty Farm in West Sussex, farm workers Jayne and Patrick Leaney had good cause to praise this outstanding border collie who, all in a night's work, faced death to save his sheep.

All had retired to bed after a busy day on the farm and the flock of some three hundred ewes with their new lambs were shut in the barn for the night.

Nipper was first to smell smoke coming from the barn, but his early warning barks may have gone unnoticed.

23. *Sheep may safely graze under the watchful eye of Nipper, the brave working sheep dog who brought 300 ewes and lambs out of a blazing barn despite injury to his lungs and feet. Nipper received the award for devotion to duty in 1985.*

The dog was insistent. But by the time Patrick and Jayne Leaney were aroused, had alerted the fire brigade and thrown on some clothes, huge clouds of choking smoke were coming out of the barn.

The terrified bleating of ewes with their new lambs was driving Nipper crazy with concern. As soon as the barn door was opened, he did not hesitate to face up to the smoke and flames which could be seen inside, in order to reach the sheep.

Self preservation is the strongest instinct in any animal and there is no way of ordering a dog, however obedient, to face such a life-threatening situation unless the animal has a very high degree of courage.

Nipper worked dilligently. He brought out as many as he could, and in spite of burnt paws and lungs filled with smoke, returned for more.

In the confusion, many desperate ewes became parted from their own lambs, and some tried to return to the barn when they heard their lambs, still trapped inside.

Nipper continued to brave the conditions, returning many times into the thick acrid smoke, until at last every one of the ewes and lambs were brought to safety. Although about ten out of the total number of some three hundred died as a result of the ordeal, every one was given the chance of safety through the perseverance of the dog.

Still Nipper's heroic act was not complete. Cows and calves were left at the other end of the burning barn, and Nipper was commanded to work on. In spite of the pain and injury he was suffering by this time, Nipper responded. All the cows and calves were driven out at last. A remarkable achievement by a dog of outstanding courage.

Police investigated the cause of the blaze which caused £50,000 worth of damage.

The incident was reported on *Coast to Coast* news television on TVS, which brought in many requests to PRO Dogs for presentation of a medal the following December.

Although the judges had no hesitation in confirming the award, one aspect concerned me.

How would this dog, used to life on a farm, who had probably never even slept inside a house, respond to a journey to London and presentation of a medal on stage with a room full of clapping admirers?

The evening was also arranged so that the dogs could sleep on show benching with kennel maids from the Dogs Home, Battersea, looking after them so that owners could enjoy their dinner in peace.

How would Nipper respond to such a strange scene? Was it fair to ask him?

After checking all these points carefully through with the owners, it was decided that Nipper had such an equable temperament that he would take it all in his stride.

This proved to be the case. Nipper was a star. He shook a now well-healed paw with anyone wanting to stroke and make a fuss of him and obviously enjoyed the whole event.

The citation of his medal for devotion to duty read: 'For bravery in overcoming the danger and fear of fire to rescue his sheep'.

―――――――― DID YOU KNOW? ――――――――

Dogs with three legs

A broken leg in a racehorse too often means the destruction of the horse. But the amputation of a leg of a dog certainly need not mean the end of active life.

In 1985 a two year old golden retriever called Sherpa had one of his back legs amputated after being crushed by a car ferry.

Vet Jim Goodwin of Paignton in Devon, who treated the dog, encouraged owner Mrs Jo Proctor not to give up hope, even though considerable surgery was needed to save Sherpa's life and leave him in fit condition.

The dog recovered quickly and ten months after the accident his owner decided to enter Sherpa in a race against over one hundred other fit dogs, all blessed with the normal compliment of four legs!

Sherpa stunned the crowd of more than 1,500 people by coming in third in his first heat and fourth in the semi-final. Many spectators had put bets on him just out of sympathy.

The race took place at Collaton St Mary in Devon on 27 July, 1985.

16. *Mountain rescue*

The first breed to spring to mind in connection with mountain rescue, must be the magnificent St Bernard.

The public image of this dog, with brandy barrel slung round his neck, is carefully fostered by the makers of Hennessy brandy who, to this day, present a trophy to the best specimen of the breed each year, as judged at Crufts dog show.

The St Bernard has a keen sense of direction and can be relied on to find mountain paths obscured by snow, even in confusing conditions of driving snow or fog. Since about as early as 1665 this breed has not only proved its worth as a path-finder, but also shown its remarkable ability in detecting human bodies, or avalanche victims, even when covered by deep snow.

Quite a different kind of working mountain rescue dog has been developed during the twentieth century following the formation of the Swiss Alpine Club at the end of World War II.

Some may think it unscrupulous to exploit dogs on the battlefields, but many different breeds from terriers to pointers and German shepherds were used by the Red Cross during both World Wars to detect and help recover injured soldiers by air scent. This led to training of more dogs for peacetime rescue purposes.

According to Angela Locke, in her book on search dogs, four German Shepherds were trained to search for avalanche victims and given to the Swiss Army. The success of these dogs led to the widespread setting up of dog training centres in the Alps after the war.

A Scotsman, Hamish MacInnes, attended one of these courses and brought back to Britain the idea of similar training courses. His own German Shepherd dogs were successfully trained, but experience and experimentation soon favoured other breeds as well, notably Border collies and Labradors.

Their work was first brought to the attention of PRO Dogs in October 1982 following reports of two children feared lost in Snowdonia.

Twelve year old Julian Smith and his sister Catherine aged

eleven had set off for a walk on 27 October from a cottage where they were staying with a family, at Nant Peris on the foot of Snowdon. They had not been seen since early afternoon. As nightfall came, two mountain rescue teams and a helicopter equipped with special lights set off to search for them. One of the teams was also aided by trained search and rescue dogs.

Gale force winds made it unsafe for the helicopter to continue to operate and soon it had to land again, leaving the twenty strong foot search team with the task of covering huge areas of bleak and craggy

mountainside. Nobody knew which direction the children had taken and Phil Benbow, searching with his black Labrador Jet, said it was like looking for a needle in a haystack.

All night the search continued, with dogs working at a distance from their handlers to cover maximum area in a methodical sweep up the mountain. Conditions were near freezing and the children had gone off wearing only wellington boots and light clothing.

At last a halt was called at 3 a.m. by the team leader. But Phil offered to search on with his ever eager dog and the brave extra effort was rewarded soon after 4 a.m. when the two children were found huddled together in a crevice 2,000ft up the peak, by Jet. The dog was excited by his find. He knew he had done what was asked of him.

24. *Mountain search dog Jet found two children, Julian and Catherine Smith, lost in Snowdonia, and received the 1983 medal for devotion to duty. Jet has been responsible for many successful rescues and is seen here at the awards dinner with Major Stafford Somerfield and his owner and handler Philip Benbow.*

The children were sobbing and Julian had been comforting his sister and assuring her help would come.

Catherine said, 'We just seemed to get higher and higher. We kept slipping and stuck our penknives into the ground to help us get a hold. It was getting darker and colder but we could not turn back because we were afraid of falling. Then we found a ditch and huddled together to keep warm. It was wonderful when the dog found us.' Both parents praised the work of the rescuers – and particularly Jet.

Moments of triumph come seldom for individual members of a mountain rescue team. Mostly it's training the dogs to the highest standards of search and find, testing to ensure these standards are maintained, and working as a team.

When the nomination for Jet to receive an award came in to the charity, the deadline of 30 September had passed. Therefore it was not possible for it to be researched and considered until the awards for the following year.

Although Jet was only two years old at the time he found the lost children, he was involved in a further two human rescues as well as a total of twenty one searching incidents before he received the PRO Dog of the Year medal for devotion to duty in 1983. Already three times a life saving hero when he stepped up on to the London stage to receive his medal, he was still a lovable and playful young dog. His black coat gleamed – until it was hidden as he demonstrated the strong jacket he had been trained to wear so that he could be winched up or down by helicopter, in emergency.

In updating information for this book some six years later, I was glad to hear that Jet was still alive and working, at the age of nine years. Shortly he would be due for honourable retirement.

However, his list of credits had by this time stretched to include over forty life-saving rescues in an average of twenty emergency call-outs every year. On each occasion he had worked with his owner and trainer Phil Benbow, in tiring and sometimes harrowing rescue.

Together they had worked in the Lockerbie air disaster in Scotland from Christmas Eve in 1988, until the following Thursday, hoping to find survivors of the outrageous terrorist bomb which had killed 178 people.

The most grisly task of all was when they were called in to recover the remains of two people who had been blown to pieces in an explosion in a factory at Penrhyndeudraeth, in Wales. The work ensured proper identification and a decent burial of the remains.

On another occasion in March 1985, Phil and Jet answered an emergency call when a group of nine ratings from the Royal Navy and two officers were lost and trapped 500 feet from the summit of Glyder Fawr in Snowdonia. In dark and freezing conditions, they had lost their path and dared not move in case they fell.

After searching for a full five hours, Jet suddenly darted off in a different direction. Clearly he had caught a scent which demanded investigation.

Guided only by the small light mounted on the dog's coat, Phil followed as fast as he could. Scrambling over the dangerous crags he was soon relieved to hear Jet give the joyous bark which meant one thing. The party had been located.

Phil called the base office on his radio and soon team members arrived with warm sleeping bags to protect the frozen ratings until the helicopter arrived to winch everyone to safety.

Eleven more people safe. And another eleven notches to carve on Jet's record card.

In addition to the Welsh team, which Phil and Jet served so well until 1990, SARDA (Search and Rescue Dog Association) has teams working independently in England, Scotland, and Ireland. The dogs have achieved such a high professional standard of work

25. *The three 1987 gold medal winners. Jacob the German shepherd with, left and right respectively, Meg and Loch, the Border collies involved in the international earthquake disaster rescue in El Salvador.*

through their rigorous training methods that they have a good record and relationship in assisting the police.

One of the tests which a dog has to pass before it can be accepted into the team is designed to ensure that dogs resist any natural urge to chase sheep. A lot of the work is on sheep grazing land – and it is important to get on well with farmers and not disturb the sheep.

Although Jet, as one of the gun dog breeds, may have had little difficulty in accepting this discipline, it can be much harder to train collies from working sheepdog stock to forget their instinctive eye for the sheep in mountain rescue work.

It can be done and many border collies are now used with great success in SARDA.

Two deserving particular mention are Loch and Meg who each received one of the medals from PRO Dogs in 1987.

Following the earthquake disaster in El Salvador in October 1986, Loch and Meg with owners David Riley and David Jones answered a call for volunteers. They became part of a team organised by the International Rescue Corps, a group united to save life anywhere in the world.

The call came for canine assistance when rescue workers realised their task was impossible without specialized sniffer dogs.

The two volunteers were not deterred, despite the knowledge that on return to Britain after the short period of rescue work, both dogs would face the stiff six month period in quarantine kennels.

They set off for their eleven hour flight, to the conditions of extreme heat, dust and rubble in which the dogs had to work. This was quite unlike any situation they were used to.

In spite of this, by using the same finding methods the dogs adapted remarkably quickly and responded to instructions.

Sound locating equipment was being used when the dogs arrived nearly a week after the horrendous quake, as rescuers refused to give up even in the face of forecasts that it was impossible for survivors to be found under so much rubble from the collapsed buildings.

Nine days after the disaster, the sound locating system showed a reading. No one dared believe there could be yet another survivor after all this time. Loch was called in. She indicated life by returning to the exact same point repeatedly. She knew there was a person down there and clearly pointed the place where further excavation was needed.

26. *Loch and Meg, the highly-trained and successful search and rescue dogs owned and handled by Mr Dave Riley and Mr Davy Jones.*

In this great International rescue, the Guatemalan fire service added their contribution by carefully continuing the digging to a depth of many feet. At last the effort was rewarded, and a man who had been buried alive for nine days was uncovered.

Speaking afterwards about his experience in working Meg, David Jones said, 'We went in blind, because we had never worked in these kind of conditions before. Unsafe buildings, the intense heat. Our interpreters who worked with us from San Salvador were most welcoming and helpful throughout our time there.

The saddest part were the children, crying because they could not locate their relatives, and who were obviously hungry.'

In many cases search and rescue dogs are retired after about ten years service. At the time Meg went out to El Salvador she was already something of a veteran. Her quarantine expenses were covered by the International Rescue Corps and it was decided to retire her when she had completed this six months period.

Pedigree Petfoods, who are always ready to help a good dog cause met Loch's expenses in quarantine. At five years of age, Loch still had many years of rescue work ahead of her, although retraining after the long period of confinement and inactivity had to be started at basic level, to get her fit again.

The two dogs were released from quarantine in April 1987, to considerable rejoicing and they were presented with their gold medals on 24 January 1988.

Both these events were widely reported in the press, so when Loch, back in harness again, was lost in the mountains shortly afterwards on Monday 8 February there was an outcry of public concern.

Loch had been called out to search in blizzard conditions for a man who was reported lost. The man was found, still alive, although unfortunately he subsequently died. But Loch was lost in a 'white out' – conditions of driving, blinding snow which make searching conditions impossibly difficult.

David Riley and a search team went out looking for her on Tuesday and again on Wednesday. PRO Dog's telephone lines were jammed with anxious enquiries from dog owners. Could they help? Had she been found?

At the time, PRO Dogs had a stand at Crufts dog show and news bulletins were posted up at regular intervals. Crowds gathered round for the latest reports. The dog who had spent most of her life in rescuing others, was now the centre of a major search party herself. Had she become disoriented by her overseas trip followed by the claustrophobic kennel conditions? Just how much is it reasonable to ask of a willing serving dog? Was the severe penalty of being shut away from the owner to whom she was devoted and the wide open spaces where she had been accustomed to working, too much?

Helicopters were brought in to search for Loch and progress was followed with as much interest as Sir Ranulph Fiennes expedition to the North and South Poles, with Bothie, reported elsewhere!

On the fourth day Loch was found. She was bewildered but thankful, just like any other rescue victim.

DID YOU KNOW?
Barry, the Saint

It is said that the St Bernard is the living symbol of strength and sacrifice.

There are conflicting reports by various authorities as to how the breed originated. Some credit the monks of the coenobite community with having created the breed themselves from dogs of Roman origin, specifically to guard the St Bernard refuge run by these monks, and provide guides for the hazardous alpine paths.

Others insist the breed is descended by a mating between German mastiffs and Pyrenean mountain dogs, while yet more breed scholars say their research shows that the Tibetan mastiff is the true ancestor of the St Bernard.

What is certainly not in dispute is that the hospice refuge of St Bernard gave name to the breed and that these dogs became the greatest friend of travellers in the Swiss Alps and on the St Bernard pass between Switzerland and Italy.

Perhaps the most famous of these early mountain rescue dogs was Barry. Between the years of 1800 and 1810 this dog alone is credited with saving the lives of forty peple.

A statue of Barry is held in the Berne Natural History Museum and is a useful guide as to the original type of dog bred for hard work and vigour. Barry was shorthaired, as were all St Bernards prior to 1830. It was not until the breed was crossed with Newfoundlands that the first longhaired St Bernards we recognise as typical today, and featured on the jacket of this book, appeared.

17. *Detecting drugs and explosives*

There can be few who would relish the title 'Sniffer of the Year' – but it seems this is a great accolade when it comes to dogs working for HM Customs and Excise Investigation division.

Nomination for a wonderful black Labrador called Brumby was received by PRO Dogs in September 1982. This came from a senior officer in Customs and Excise, looking for wider recognition of the valuable work done by the best of these dogs.

Brumby was due for retirement at the age of ten-and-a-half years, and it was felt that a medal would be a fitting final tribute to a dog with a great record.

Born on 6 April 1972, Brumby's future was planned even before he was born. But it had certainly not been planned for him to become a Customs sniffer dog. Brumby was bred by that distinguished gentleman, Derek Freeman, a past breeding manager for the Guide Dogs for the Blind Association.

Brumby's sire was Guidewell Hansa, a stud dog out of one of the most successful guide dog brood bitches of all time. Her name was Harmony and she was remarkable because she worked successfully herself as a guide dog before being called into the breeding programme to pass on her excellent qualities.

Incidentally, it would be impossible for this to happen today, because all dogs are neutered before training begins.

Brumby's dam was a Labrador called Sedak. She was donated to the Guide Dogs for the Blind as a brood bitch. She had some field trials blood in her breeding and the success rate of her puppies in qualifying as guide dogs was not high.

Brumby, too, failed at assessment time when he came back to Guide Dogs after his puppy walking days. But he was a remarkable dog and still stands out in the memory of Derek Freeman, despite all the many dogs which have been assessed by him and passed through his hands.

'A striking looking animal,' Mr Freeman recalled. 'Spirited and

27. Brumby protects London from illicit drugs! Seen here by the Thames, this Labrador with a wonderful nose worked for H.M. Customs and Excise, Investigation Division, and was awarded PRO Dog's 1982 medal for devotion to duty for his record 210 successful drug detections worth over £4m.

reminded me of a black stallion. He was certainly a bright dog. Liked to use his nose but that isn't what we need in a Guide dog. He was just so exuberant and wanted to be on the go all the time'.

So Brumby was given the boot – and found a new career, right under his nose. In October 1973 he went to the RAF Police to be trained as a search dog. Terry McHaffie, another well known figure in the world of dogs, was chief training officer and was soon greatly impressed by the dog's aptitude for drug detection.

Drugs such as cannabis and heroin have a distinctive smell and it's child's play for a dog with its natural keen scenting ability to detect the smell, even in minute quantities and if carefully concealed in boxes, furniture – or even in the tyres of vehicles.

Success lies in playing a game of hide and seek with drug scented objects and rewarding the dog when it finds and barks to indicate where the haul is hidden. There is no truth in suggestions that it is necesary to first get dogs hooked on the drugs they are expected to find. On one notable occasion when a dog did manage to find and swallow a large lump of cannabis, he was in cloud cuckoo land for days and unable to work. To allow the dogs to become addicted would be self defeating.

Brumby served with the Royal Navy in Portsmouth until March 1976 and during this time gave a demonstration of his abilities to a party of Officers, one of whom was HRH Prince Charles.

Using dogs for drug detection by HM Customs and Excise was revolutionary in 1976 when the idea was tried in England. And who better to pioneer the scheme than Brumby? He was teamed with Vic Jones in May of that year when Vic had been first off to answer an advertisement to form the new Customs dog section.

Formerly Vic Jones had been a flight sergeant and senior instructor with the Police dog Training Flight, and he was to grow so fond of Brumby that when at last retirement day came for the dog, Vic bought him out of the service to ensure a happy discharge for his good pal.

In early years they were paired with Jim Morley and a yellow Labrador called Brandy, a year older than Brumby, to start the service into action.

The first two years of service were so successful that the number of working dogs was increased to sixteen by 1980. Vic Jones always claimed that Brumby was a super dog and I have to admit that PRO Dogs had never up to that time received quite as many glowing testimonials and news cuttings in support of any other dog nomination. 'Dog found drug in cushions: nurse gaoled', 'Brumby, best drug finder in country', 'Sniffer dog smells out drug runners', 'Brumby's no Dope', 'Drug dog hero: Sixteen arrested', and

'Brumby scents heroin in false-front boots' all make intriguing reading.

Three years earlier, his nomination for a medal had not quite succeeded. By 1982 he was undeniably a winner. He had made 210 drug detections to a total value of nearly £4,000,000. He had detected drugs concealed in all the most unlikely places; car wheel arches, tyres, built inside furniture or generators and concealed on the person. He had opened the eyes of the service still further to the ingenuity of the smuggler. He even detected drugs masked and hidden by a powerful smelling antiseptic cream. He had discovered herbal cannabis, cannabis resin, cannabis oil and heroin in huge quantities. No illicit drug smuggler was safe from Brumby's incredible nose.

Due to this great success, at his retirement the workforce of dogs had been expanded to thirty three dogs. And maybe several of these would be needed to replace him.

They said Brumby was a workaholic. Even off duty, he never could resist search duties, although mostly then his attention would turn to Polo mints. He was very fond of them and never forgot his occasional early peppermint rewards when he started training.

A great dog. And a pioneer of yet another way in which dogs can help people. This time in the fight against international drug trafficking.

Dogs can be trained with equal success to detect TNT and other explosives. Once again it is the distinctive odour which the dog can detect.

Black Labrador Jason was trained for Army duties. It was his job to detect the lethal bombing devices planted by the IRA and give warning in time to save the lives of soldiers on foot patrols in Northern Ireland.

Jason's frienziedly wagging tail was the signal that he had made a find, so that the men could immediately dive for cover.

Jason had been taught to please his handler by making these finds, and each time he succeeded in doing so, his tail would wag in pleasurable anticipation. In the early days he would have received a titbit, but as he became accustomed to the 'game', just the knowledge that he had achieved what was asked of him and the pat and fuss ahead from his satisfied handler would be enough to start that tail wagging.

He was like Pavlov's dogs, taught to salivate in anticipation of food at the sound of a gong.

Above: *These Newfoundlands are strong enough to save the life of a drowning man. They can be taught to dive into water from cliff tops and provide spectacular water-rescue.*

Right: *After his brother died, Bernie Winters took a 'Saint' as his stage partner – with great success. Schnorbitz the St Bernard, won the PRO Dog of the year 'Oscar' for pet of the year in 1986.*

Above: *Toastmaster Jimmy Meredith announces that dinner is served to two special medal-winning guests, Nipper and Oscar, at the grand London event to celebrate the best of British dogs in 1985. Still held every year.*

Above: *Pasha the German shepherd won PRO Dog's award for life saving in 1989 after protecting his owner Nikola Stedul from a terrifying assassination attempt, in Scotland.*

28. *Ben the brave yellow labrador retriever search dog might well have been nominated to receive an award if he had survived. Sadly, both Ban and his handler, Corporal Derak Hayes, aged 28, died in May 1988, killed by an IRA bomb in South Armagh, Northern Ireland.*

One day in July 1989, the friendly Jason was on duty with the Royal Hampshire Regiment in Londonderry, when that wagging tail saved the lives of four soldiers.

Suddenly Jason sniffed the air and walked towards a dustbin on the Letterkenny Road. Frenziedly the tail wagged and the alarmed soldiers dashed for cover. Two of the soldiers received minor injuries as 150lbs of explosives detonated by remote control. Two more were unhurt.

Jason was blown into the air and suffered concussion, but soon made a recovery. His handler said: 'Jason is a real hero and we are all proud of him, I'm just relieved he was up and about again so soon'.

This was the second occasion Jason had been responsible for a livesaving action. In 1988 the five year old dog had sniffed out a Republican arms dump in Londonderry.

The army flew Jason to London to receive his PRO Dog of the Year gold medal for devotion to duty on 17 December, 1989.

DID YOU KNOW?

Dogs Shoot their Owners

During 1989 not one, but two dogs actually managed to shoot their owners.

The first report from near Bathurst, Sydney, Australia stated that Graham Williams was nursing a flesh wound after his dog knocked over a loaded rifle in the family car. Source of this information is *The Mail on Sunday* 20 October 1989.

The second report, from *The Times* of 24 October, was rather more serious. It concerned a Swedish elk-hunting expedition in Stockholm which ended in tragedy when a slaughterhouse worker involved in the hunt was killed – shot by his own dog who stood on the trigger of his best friend's rifle.

Ironic that a man who spent his life killing animals should die in such an untimely manner himself.

IV

CHILDREN AND DOGS

29. Zac the dobermann saved the life of his eleven-year-old owner, David Dudding, when the boy was in danger of drowning in rough sea currents.

18. Zak the Dobermann repays a debt

The sad fact about Zak the dobermann was that at the age of eight months he was an unwanted dog. Like many young dogs before him, and since, he had grown too big and strong for his owners, who gave up, deciding they could no longer cope. There is no law to prevent the untimely destruction of dogs – whose only crime is not to have been properly understood and planned for – and huge numbers of them are killed with appalling regularity.

That was to have been Zak's fate.

Mrs Cathy Dudding of West Lothian in Scotland took pity on him. She saved the owner the £12 the vet was going to charge to put him down and she took Zak into her home, where he soon became an obedient and loving companion for her two sons.

Very quickly the dog formed a bond with eleven year old David and always waited eagerly to welcome him from school.

In the school holidays in August 1982, Mrs Dudding took both her sons for a day treat to Lossiemouth.

The boys enjoyed playing in the water, swimming and splashing about happily for some time. Zak, preferring not to get wet unless he had to, watched keenly from the waters edge, ready to bound up in greeting the second David emerged.

Gradually David ventured further and further out and quite suddenly, unnoticed by Cathy Dudding, a freak current caught David up and swept him away. Such treacherous currents are known to occur at that notorious part of the mouth of the estuary once every few years.

Zak was on his feet and into the water at once. He barked a warning but Cathy did not appreciate the danger. She thought Zak was asking her to play a game.

David was rapidly being swept further away and out to sea. If he was crying for help, only Zak heard him. But the faithful dog needed no urging. He was out and swimming strongly in the water.

At last, the dog's valiant efforts were noticed by two willing would-be rescuers attracted by Zak's barks. They entered the water to help. But Zak was by this time far ahead of them and had nearly reached the desperate boy. Another moment, and they were together.

David grabbed thankfully at Zak.

The two swimmers, now approaching, could see that for a moment it seemed that boy and dog were going under together. After what seemed an age, boy and dog could be seen floating on the surface again. Zak was already clearly making a brave effort to strike out for the shore. David was calmer now and soon they were swimming hard together against the strong current. Slight progress was gradually being made in the exhausting conditions.

Even when the two swimers approached, David would not let go of his dog. Zak was his lifeline, and he knew it.

At last they managed to escape from the treacherous current and for the last stage of the journey were pulled into the shore by anxious helpers, by this time almost unconscious.

30. *Zak the dobermann received the PRO Dog of the Year gold medal for life-saving in 1982. Seen here with young David Dudding and Mr Jack Easson who presented the award.*

Although physically sick and totally exhausted, neither boy nor dog took long to recover.

This was not the first time Zak had proved a hero. A few months earlier, the family had been staying in Edinburgh with Mrs Dudding's sister when the whole house was gutted by a fire. This had started at about 2 a.m. as a result of a faulty television set.

That time the whole family of five had been alerted by Zak's warning barks, which awoke them. They all escaped and reached safety in time.

Zak received his gold medal award for lifesaving on the same stage and on the same night that Brumby and Bothie were honoured with medals for devotion and duty and pet of the year. Zak's medal was appropriately presented by Jack Easson, who also hails from Scotland and represented Wilsons of Dundee who supported the medals in the earliest years between 1979–83. The weekly canine publication *Dog World* has supported the awards since then.

When Brian Imber, master of ceremonies, interviewed Mrs Cathy Dudding, she said: 'When I saved Zak, I didn't know that this was a deed which would save the lives of my family. Zak is a great dog. We all love him'.

DID YOU KNOW?

Childhood Influence

If there is a dog in the family when you are a child, the chances that you will choose to own one later in life are greatly increased.

The type of dog you like and choose is also likely to be influenced by early family experience, according to a study carried out by Dr James Serpell in 1981.

Books and films also undoubtedly have an influence on choice and the films about Lassie greatly increased the demand for rough collies. Rin Tin Tin was probably the most famous German shepherd film-star dog of them all and certainly increased the call for dogs 'like him'.

Disney dogs have been loved by children of several generations and following the popularity of '101 Dalmatians', Kennel Club registrations dramatically increased.

This isn't always good news for the dogs.

Even television commercials have an effect and the Dulux paint promotions had the unfortunate effect of over popularizing the Old English sheepdog. The breed looks so lovable that suddenly everyone wanted one, without appreciating that these dogs demand lots of care and exercise and daily attention to the shaggy coat.

Soon the breed rescue societies had difficulty in coping with all the cast-off dogs.

Knowledge of the needs of different types of dog picked up almost unknowingly in childhood is useful preparation towards a successful man and dog partnership in the future.

19.   *Substitute dogs*

Perhaps the most enjoyable nominations to receive are the ones from children who would like nothing better than a medal for their own dog.

But although dog ownership is highest in Britain amongst families with children at home, there are still many children who yearn to have a dog but cannot do so. Where both parents are out at work, or where there is a single working parent, it simply is not fair to have a dog and leave it alone for long lonely hours.

Perhaps that is why dogs featured regularly on television programmes become so popular. Substitute dogs, for people who cannot have one of their own.

Typical is a letter received in beautifully careful handwriting from nine year old Jessica McConnell, in 1981. It said:

'Dear PRO Dogs,
I would like Goldie of *Blue Peter* to get a medal. She is such a special dog because she is so well mannered, and you can tell she has such kind ways. For all the children who have not got a dog, she is OUR dog and our pet to share
From Jessica'

Goldie had been mentioned often enough to the judges, most of whom visit schools as volunteers with the caring dog ownership campaign, for them to recognise that this would be a choice to please many young people.

Dogs so often deserve to be rewarded in an appropriate way, perhaps just with a pat or a game, but it is good when children notice this and disappointing not to be able to offer an award to a child who writes:

'If it wasn't for our dog Bess, our house would be empty when I get home from school. Bess is pleased to see me and she wags her tail, so it doesn't seem lonely at all. Please give the medal to Bess. Mum says we can easily come to get it. Love from Caroline.'

31. *Nine-year-old Jessica McConnell successfully nominated Goldie, the BBC Blue Peter dog, for a medal as pet of the year in 1981 – 'for all the children who have not got a dog, because she is our dog, to share'. Seen here with Ann Groom, Mr Jack Easson and the author (left).*

But sadly Caroline's letter goes on one side. Bess has done no more than hundreds of thousands of other dogs – and at least she has an appreciative owner.

Goldie, on the other hand, is something of a public figure. She had been carefully groomed by Biddy Baxter, programme editor at the time, to feature in the lives of the huge eager audience at their peak viewing time. 'Goldie is always the perfect lady and no matter what the occasion, whether out on location filming with the *Blue Peter* cameras, or in the studio under the hot bright lights, Goldie in her calm steady way is always very much part of what is going on'.

You can almost hear Biddy Baxter talking, in Jessica's letter!

Goldie was selected for the programme by Derek Freeman of the Guide Dogs for the Blind Association. She joined the programme at seven weeks of age and spent her home life with Simon Groom one of the programme presenters and his wife Ann.

Goldie followed in the good animal tradition of this favourite BBC long-running programme, which started with a top famous mongrel called Petra, now written into the annals of BBC history.

This black and brown dog, with prick ears and an intelligent expression entered the stage in 1962 and made a reported 1,192 appearances. She retired in June 1977 and died later that year at nearly fifteen years of age. When she died, tears were probably shed by millions of children and a bronze statue of her stands inside the main gates of Television centre to this day.

The children really had been involved in her life. They had chosen her mate (Bellman, a beagle, who actually failed to sire her puppies) and Moss a Shetland sheepdog, who succeeded because Petra much preferred him. They also chose the names for her nine puppies, including Patch who was retained and joined the programme.

Goldie had a big reputation to live up to, but children change little in their natural delight for animals, and Goldie fulfilled every expectation.

When invited to receive her PRO Dog of the year award as pet of the year in 1981 she was just over three years of age and already the proud mother of five puppies. These were named, by the viewing children, of course. By popular vote they were called Sandy, Prince, Buster, Henry and Diana. At the time of her award, an estimated 8 million children turned on regularly to watch her.

Jessica McConnell was thrilled when she was invited to the dinner and asked to present the medal to Goldie, on the stage in London. She then faced up very well to the questions put to her by Brian Imber, the master of ceremonies, and explained why she thought the medal should be given.

'We used to have a dog,' she said, 'but he got very old, and died. We miss him but we can't have another dog now. Goldie is my dog to share. And I love her,' she said simply. Spontaneously she put an arm round the dog's neck, much to the approval of the clicking camera men.

Jessica also appeared with her original letter on the following *Blue Peter* programme. Her school friends were impressed for several days.

Other media dogs also received mass nominations, and the next one to receive the pet of the year medal was Oscar.

Not many newshounds are actually dogs – but Oscar proved an interesting exception. For several years, the independent television Central *Newshound* programme revolved round the exploits and adventures of this very appealing German wirehaired pointer.

Although this regional programme had a comparatively modest viewer rating, compared with the networked BBC *Blue Peter* programme, Oscar quickly established himself as a firm favourite. As in the case of Goldie, the viewers were invited to choose his name.

While viewers may have felt that Oscar was, to a degree at least, 'their' dog, home for Oscar was in Little Heywood, Staffordshire, with Celia Walker. This good and tireless person seldom allowed Oscar to refuse an invitation to open a fete for a good cause.

In 1985, Oscar became a good cause himself, by giving his name to the 'Oscar Appeal'. This was designed to raise funds for children in need of special equipment at Birmingham's Children's Hospital. Thousands of pounds poured in, every time Oscar's delightful hangdog expression was exposed to public gaze and soon the children were begging Oscar to visit them in hospital.

So Oscar became a P.A.T. dog. Pets As Therapy (P.A.T.) is a scheme started by PRO Dogs in 1983 and it involves volunteers offering to take their dogs on regular visits to people in hospitals, hospices, homes for children or the elderly. Anywhere, in fact, that people are shut away from the everyday world and miss the diverting and pleasing companionship of animals.

Not every dog is suitable as a registered P.A.T. dog. Before they are accepted, all dogs offered have to show that they are really friendly, not just to their owners but to anyone else who may want to stroke or pat them. They don't exactly have to sit an examination, but they do have to pass a temperament test.

Oscar passed with flying colours and soon had his official P.A.T. disc to wear on his collar.

One day when Celia and Oscar were visting the Children's Hospital in Birmingham, they saw the distressed parents of a 12 year old boy who was very sick and had been in a coma for some days. Recognising the dog from the *Newshound* programme, the boy's mother suddenly had an idea: 'Would you please, please come and see Neil,' she begged, 'we are so worried about him. He loved Oscar when he saw him on TV, and it might do him good.'

The ward sister was doubtful, but finally agreed it could do no harm, and they all went up to the ward. 'Look who has come to see you, Neil' said his mother, with warmth and pleasure in her voice. 'It's Oscar. You remember Oscar, don't you?'

The child did not stir. At first it seemed he had not heard. Patiently they waited, all joining in and telling the young boy that Oscar was waiting there to see him.

Oscar put his head on the bed. He nudged Neil's hand. Maybe the combined sound of the voices and the feel of the dog's coat somehow managed to penetrate his consciousness. He opened his eyes, and his mother held her breath. 'Oscar,' said Neil, with immediate recognition. And everyone knew that Neil was well on the way to recovery.

Oscar also proved himself a dog in a million by opening his own bank account with Barclays Bank, under his pawmark, so as to pay out generous sums from his Appeal Fund for the needy.

Even a dog like Oscar needs something to snap at occasionally – adequately provided for in the programme by his 'growl-of-the-week'. This gave a chance to have a hard dig at any overbearing authority or point out any unreasonable bureaucratic decision which was making life miserable for Oscar's best friend, the under-dog. Or in his case, the underman.

Cold scientists may frown at such anthropomorphism, but it is better to endow animals with human characteristics and feelings and treat them kindly and with respect due to all animal life, than to delude ourselves that man stands alone as the only animal which matters. Perhaps the occasional small indulgence of the *Newshound* kind can be justified on the grounds that it is a good defence against cruelty. If animals are seen as 'lovable' they are less likely to be harmed, or even callously abandoned by their owners.

Beliefs which were rife in the sixteenth and seventeenth centuries about creatures created only to serve man, the supreme animal, are fortunately no longer so widely held today. In that period, some even persuaded themselves that animals were unable to feel pain and that when dogs cried out as they were beaten, they could feel nothing and were behaving only like an automatic alarm clock which responds when a spring has been touched.

True reverence for all life and life-forms puts us in our rightful place in the universe and if building the status of animals helps to encourage us to value and care more about them, what's wrong with that?

Another good image-building dog was Schnorbitz. She followed on by popular demand as pet of the year medal winner in 1986.

The St Bernard is a big animal immediately commanding attention for his great size. The gentle temperament which should, and nearly always does, go with it makes him especially attractive. However, a St Bernard is not a dog to go in for without a great deal of consideration – and is certainly not suitable for anyone who has an aversion to a fair amount of dog-slobber!

Schnorbitz I (who was replaced by Schnorbitz II, when she died in June 1987) was a St Bernard, and her fame was greatly enhanced by her well known owner, the comedian Bernie Winters. Or was it Bernie's image which was promoted by Schnorbitz? The fact is they made a great team and certainly Bernie Winters was not the

32. *Bernie Winters' St Bernard, Schnorbitz, was interested to meet Chloë, this very small chihuahua P.A.T. hospital dog, owned by Mrs Kandy Bate, at the awards dinner in 1986.*

first to use to advantage the increased popularity which comes from close association with an appealing dog.

There is no doubt that the combined Bernie–Schnorbitz team gave the appealing note to the Thames television series, *It's Bernie*, which was built upon for the following series *Whose Baby?* Schnorbitz was tolerant in the extreme and could always be relied on to behave well in the studios and wherever Bernie was called on location.

Perhaps her greatest popularity came in the winter pantomime season when she appeared on the best known provincial theatre stages in Manchester, Birmingham and other regions. The children lived for the moment when Bernie called up to fifty of them onto the stage with Schnorbitz. There the accommodating dog would be subjected to mass petting, stroking and some pulling about. All of this she lapped up with pleasure.

Nevertheless, it could have been an ordeal for an animal to put up with twice daily performances and so many children. Only a star personality dog like Schnorbitz would take it in her stride.

It was particularly testing for her when she started to suffer pain from hip dysplasia in 1985. The skilled attention of the Royal Veterinary College put her right again with a two-night stay in hospital and she soon recovered.

That year she was able to attend the Duchess of Kent's Christmas party held for the war veterans at Buckingham Palace, where it is rumoured she got on well with the corgis. Schnorbitz's constant home companions were Ella a German Shepherd dog and Putzi a tiny Yorkshire terrier. So she was accustomed to the antics of smaller dogs.

When the day came for Schnorbitz to receive her PRO Dog of the year medal as pet of the year, she was besieged by photographers. One of them insisted that she was photographed with a small Chihuahua belonging to Kandy Bate, one of the hostesses that night. 'Please don't!' said an agitated spectator, 'one bite, and the little dog will disappear.' Schnorbitz treated the remark with the contempt which it deserved, and the tiny dog sat safely on one enormous front paw, for the benefit of the papers next day.

Remarkable to think that both these dogs had descended from a single primitive stock. One weighed less than 4lb, the other over 100lb, produced by a combination of chance mutation and skilled selective breeding over countless generations.

In May 1987, the medal winning dogs from the previous awards dinner were invited to the celebrity start of 'Walkover Britain' in Hyde Park, London. This is the main charity fund-raising event of the year for PRO Dogs and each year these canine favourites are asked to put their best foot forward in support of the event.

Schnorbitz duly attended, along with Bernie Winters and his wife Siggi. Also a six month old St Bernard puppy. She was being groomed as understudy for Schnorbitz and was already designated Schnorbitz II.

Although she seemed well on the day, and once again obligingly posed for photographs, sadly this was to be Schnorbitz's last public appearance.

When Bernie and Siggi were out walking with her on Friday 19 June, a few weeks afterwards, she suddenly stumbled and fell. They rushed home for a blanket to carry her back and to take her to the vet. But it was too late. The great hearted animal was dead. And her soft-hearted master wept like a child.

DID YOU KNOW?
Raising Better Children

According to the noted paediatric consultant and psychologist Dr Lee Salk of Chicago, a family pet can help children become better people in a number of ways.

Dogs help people to have a good image of themselves and self esteem and confidence are vital for everyone, but especially the developing child. A welcoming dog, always pleased to see you, is very good for making people feel they matter.

The majority of crime is caused by people with low, or very low, self esteem.

By learning to recognise and understand differences between pets and themselves, children can learn to adapt to differences among people. They can also learn the pleasures of sharing which is especially important if the child has no brothers or sisters.

Children can learn the importance of loyalty through enjoying the devotion and protection given naturally to them by the family dog. By using the pet to illustrate this value, the child can learn to cherish it and develop loyalty to their own friends.

I have always considered that to be told you are behaving like an animal is more of a compliment than an insult.

20. *Saved from fire*

A number of children and adults owe their lives to the early warning of fire risk by the family dog, and Leah Kramer is one of them.

One cold night in January 1985, six year old Leah and her mother Sandra Kramer had turned in for an early night, when husband Michael was away at a meeting.

Harvey the Basset hound was asleep downstairs as usual, but like every good guard dog he had a constant ear open for any threat or danger.

Suddenly Mrs Kramer was awakened by the plaintive howling and whining of Harvey. At first she took no notice, thinking he was just a nuisance and would soon be quiet again. But Harvey knew

33. *Leah Kramer, aged five, with her faithful basset hound Harvey who saved her and her mother, Mrs Sandra Kramer, when fire broke out in their home in Devon.*

he must raise the alarm and became frantic in his efforts to attract her attention. She heard thumping and banging as he rushed about, unable to reach either her or Leah, turning over the kitchen stools as he went. Its sounded as if there was a wild party going on downstairs and at last she sleepily got out of bed.

As soon as she opened her bedroom door, she saw that the landing was full of thick smoke. The door of Leah's room was open and it too was full of smoke. Hastily putting on shoes and dressing gowns, they collected Harvey and made their escape to call the fire brigade from a neighbour's house. From outside it could be seen that smoke was billowing everwhere, caused by a log which had rolled out of the fire onto the carpet.

Sandra Kramer said, 'If it hadn't been for Harvey, we should have been cut off. The fire would have reached the stairs and we should never have been able to get down them in time.'

Fortunately by getting the call in to the brigade quickly they were able to get the fire under control before too much damage was done, and the 250 year old cottage was saved from any struc-tural damage. The station officer confirmed that but for Harvey, mother and daughter would certainly have been at risk of suffoca-tion or being burnt alive.

On 30 November 1986 Harvey travelled from his home in Laun-ceston, Devon, with the Kramer family to receive his medal for life saving. The appealing hound with his long silky ears and hangdog expression, accompanied by the lovely little Leah, stole the scene. 'Harvey saved my life, you know', she told the audience, 'and I really love him'.

The nine year old dog deserved his moment of fame and the family were to be especially grateful for the photographs taken on the occasion and the presentation of a portrait of Harvey, by artist Doreen Vincent.

Just a few weeks after the portrait was presented, Harvey was reportedly run over by the school bus and killed, when he was taken one day to meet Leah from school.

This tragedy for the family was hopefully made a little easier for them to bear by the portrait and the photographs given to them as a result of the award as a fitting memorial to a loyal dog.

There are of course many deserving dogs who never receive an award and this is because they have not been nominated to receive one or because the information sent to PRO Dogs to support a nomination is so sparse that it is impossible for the researchers to follow.

Throughout the years Iain Gordon, who was with the BBC in London for many years before joining PRO Dogs as a trustee, has worked with me to research all these reports. Iain has consistently spent hours of his time, year after year, to help prepare for the annual grand celebration of brave dogs. If dogs ever get together to present medals for devotion, no doubt Iain Gordon will be high on the list.

Researching reports has led us to all parts of Britain, including Northern Ireland. On one occasion, I remember insisting to my long suffering husband Peter that we should spend our summer holiday in North Wales so that I could do the necessary research on the SARDA dogs in North Wales, to support a nomination for Phil Benbow's wonderful search dog Jet.

A dog who deserved to be in the running in 1983, was a black Labrador named Trooper. This dog was reported in the *Western Daily Press* and the *Evening Chronicle*, circulating in the Bath area, as having saved the life of a ten week old baby when fire swept through the home of the Curtis family in Farmborough.

Fire started when a television set exploded in the living room of the house at 19 The Mead, which is the middle of a terrace of three.

Mrs Maureen Curtis was upstairs at the time, with her two year old son Darren, but the new baby Ian was in the room where the fire started.

Many dogs are protective to young children sensing that like puppies they are vulnerable young things. As a general rule, however, it is not wise to leave a dog alone with very young children as not every dog can be completely relied upon for perfect temperament.

Clearly Trooper was an ideal dog. When Mrs Curtis raced downstairs, she found him braving the heat and lying across the baby and protecting him. Ian was unhurt, but Trooper suffered burns and scorching of his coat. The dog was so concerned for the baby, that Mrs Curtis had difficulty in insisting that he moved, so as to take them out to safety.

The fire completely wrecked the downstairs of their home as well as the upstairs furnishings, despite prompt help from the neighbours who fought to keep the blaze under control until the fire brigade arrived.

'Trooper saved my baby,' said Mrs Curtis. 'He is a very good dog.'

A family in the Midlands also had cause for gratitude to their Staffordshire bull terrier for rescuing two year old Alex Jackson from a dangerous situation in March 1983.

The protective instinct of Bess, a young dark brindle and white dog, was immediately alerted when toddler Alex pushed an armchair against a lighted gas fire in the room. The dog stood between the child and the chair which quickly started to leak molten, choking foam. When Alex's mother, Denise, reached the room, already full of fumes, the dog was nudging the child away from the chair. The dog actually had the arm of the child held very gently in his mouth as a young pup would be held, without marking the arm at all, and was clearly making towards the door. Mrs Jackson said, 'I just grabbed Alex and ran out of the room, slamming the door shut. Bess was just marvellous.'

The house was so badly damaged that the family had to move out until repairs were completed.

This report was received from the Staffordshire bull terrier breed club which is always concerned for the welfare of the breed and to ensure that despite reports of fearless fighting by this brave breed, it is appreciated that these dogs are generally reliable and gentle with people. The club presented Bess with a specially made collar and lead.

On Saturday 20 August 1988 yet another family, this time in Basingstoke, Hampshire, escaped death thanks to their pet dog.

At 3 a.m. the Jakes family were roused by dobermann Rocky, pounding up the stairs. He barked the alarm when the kitchen of their home in Milton Close started to blaze.

Upstairs forty-eight year old Owen Jakes and his wife Nancy, and three of their children, were asleep. Rocky's warning enabled them all to escape alive, although Mrs Jakes, had to be rushed to hospital suffering from smoke inhalation.

Later Mr Jakes said, 'We are all just happy to be alive – thanks to Rocky. He was magic'.

Small dogs can be just as useful as large ones when it comes to fire warning and Oz, a Yorkshire terrier, illustrates this very well.

On 23 April 1989, Mr Brian Cooper's wife and three children were asleep in bed when he returned home.

Feeling hungry, he decided to cook himself some chips. However, after putting on the chip pan he sat down on the sitting room settee and fell asleep.

Soon afterwards the pan caught fire.

Oz the terrier recognised the need for action and barked and jumped up onto the settee, licking Mr Cooper's face persistently until he had managed to rouse him. Waking his family upstairs quickly he then managed to escape with them from the burning house through a broken window.

Firemen from Hemsworth, Yorkshire, said the Coopers had been lucky to escape death and once again the toast for livesaving was to a dog. This time, a very small one.

The largest number of nominations for gold medals come in as a result of fire in the home, where a dog has raised the alarm in time for people to escape. Many are received every year. Occasionally dogs raise the alarm when there is fire in a neighbouring house or flat, so this good work is not limited to families which own dogs.

But how many cases must there be which go unrecognised or unreported? Obviously PRO Dogs hears only of a tiny percentage, as most people would not know or think to nominate their dog for an award.

During 1987 in Britain, the fire brigade dealt with 63,200 fires in dwellings in which 710 people died and 9,476 were injured.

In this single short chapter, five family pets were responsible for saving the lives of nine children and five adults.

Clearly dogs may be a major source of benefit to the community in terms of early fire warning, alone.

DID YOU KNOW?

Fear of Dogs

'Children and dogs, happy together, make for a better tomorrow,' according to HSH The Princess Antoinette of Monaco, who is the President of PRO Dogs.

The Princess supports school visits in Britain by volunteer members of the charity with the 'Dogs Deserve Better People' education campaign.

But along with the campaign goes a questionnaire as a feed back on how many children have a dog at home, where and how it was acquired – and how many children have a fear of dogs.

When the survey began in about 1983, approximately two per cent of children said they feared dogs. But the more recent media hype regarding dangers from dogs seems to have had an effect. In 1989 as many as six per cent of children expressed such a fear.

All these children are invited to come and meet a reliable, friendly registered P.A.T. dog at the end of such visits. It is rewarding to watch a hesitant child slowly gain confidence and sometimes end up stroking the dog with obvious pleasure. It is likely that in this way many a threatened phobia is prevented from developing into a serious difficulty.

The children are always warned to ask the owner before they stroke the dog.

---

21.   *Kidnapper foiled*

Max was born in a hedgerow. His mother was an abandoned mongrel, heavily in whelp and she had made a cosy nest, well dug out of the ground and lined with grass, under a hedge.

The bitch and her puppies were discovered during haymaking and the villagers of Kippax in Yorkshire, near where she was found, took pity on her and did their best to find them all good homes.

In Britain today packs of dogs are seen far less often than they were twenty years earlier. In answer to the demands of society, the dog wardens and dogs homes between them have rounded up most stray dogs, and destroyed the majority.

It is comparatively rare for unwanted dogs to escape detection long enough to revert to living and fending for themselves, even in remote areas, and no easy job for a bitch on her own to find enough food to bring up a litter.

Judith Harrison and her husband Joseph were residents of Kippax and it would certainly not be true to say that they wanted a dog. They did not. But they did feel it was up to them to help out by providing a home for one of the puppies. So they took in Max.

Eleven year old Vicky Clark, Judith Harrison's daughter by her previous marriage, was very pleased about the puppy and soon a good rapport grew between them. She delighted in watching Max grow and develop and in teaching him to sit and behave as a good dog should.

Vicky also felt comfort in talking to Max. It is not always easy for young people to cope with changes in domestic circumstances, and maybe Max helped her.

But Max was to prove himself an even more valuable friend one evening when she returned in an unhappy mood after a visit away from home. Vicky called out to her family that she was taking Max out and was off, before anyone could stop or talk to her.

With Max on his lead they set off down the well lit High Street

34. *Max the mongrel who foiled kidnappers in Kippax, Yorkshire, when they attempted to make eleven-year-old Vicky Clark get into a car with them. Max was given a home by the family out of pity, but he has more than repaid their kindness.*

and turned off into a quiet road near the school. Vicky became aware of a car drawing up slowly. The driver enquired about directions and then asked her if she would like to get in the back of the car. She was at first dubious and then alarmed, but her terror grew when a man wearing a balaclava mask jumped out of the back of the car and told her to get in. She backed away and the man grabbed her, putting his hand over her mouth to keep her quiet.

Max immediately sprang into action. Although he had never bitten anyone in his young life, he was certainly not going to stand by when he could sense danger to Vicky. He promptly surprised the man by sinking his teeth into his calf. The man let out a curse, kicked out at the dog and hit Vicky. By this time Max was growling angrily. He managed to catch the man's hand, and bit that deeply as well, giving Vicky a valuable moment in which to dodge away and race for home as fast as she could while the cowardly attacker and his accomplice made off in the car.

Vicky arrived home in a state of breathless terror, and Joseph Harrison immediately sent for the police. Max arrived moments later. He had blood on his coat and at first it was thought that he had been injured when the man lunged out at him. However it was only good evidence that the dog had scored well against Vicky's attacker.

The police commended the bravery of Max. Detective Inspector Terry Rider said: 'It was a very determined attempt to kidnap Vicky and obviously premeditated. They could have tried it before and could strike again'. He added: 'Vicky was very shaken but she's plucky with plenty of character and kept her wits about her'.

Vicky's stepfather Joseph said, 'Max is just a pet and Vicky is inseparable from him. He's been no sort of guard dog and normally doesn't even bark if someone comes to the door. But he must have realised what was happening and now he's very much on guard if a stranger approaches the house'.

The story was well covered in the *Daily Mirror* on 3 September 1988 and resulted in a number of nominations coming in just before the annual closing date at the end of the month.

Vicky was glad to hear that Max had been selected and she came to London with her family for the medal presentation on 18 December.

Next morning Max was a national hero with announcements on national news and in the press, and Vicky and Max were invited to

the TV am programme *Good Morning Britain* and regional programmes in the Yorkshire area.

It is strange but perhaps not surprising that many rescued dogs
repay in full measure the debt they owe to people who give them a
chance and Judith and Joseph Harrison had good cause to be
thankful they gave a home to the poor little unwanted mongrel
found by chance under the hedge.

35. 'What did you get your medal for, then, Sammy?' Max the terrier seems to be asking.
Both dogs were rewarded for the intelligence and bravery at the 1988 PRO Dog of the Year
awards ceremony in London.

DID YOU KNOW?

Dog Psychologist

Although dogs adapt probably better than any other animal to the constraints of domestication, some dogs certainly suffer from the demands of society. Male dogs like to lift their legs and scent mark their territory – in the home. They can't be allowed to do so.

Dogs with a strong will may opt to become number 'One' in the pecking order and dominate the owner, unless prevented by the knowledgeable owner. There have been cases of dogs insisting on sleeping on the bed with the wife, growling every time the husband also tries to get into bed!

One man who has spent a lifetime in study of people and animals and now spends his time sorting out difficult relationships between dogs and their owners is psychologist Dr Roger Mugford. His efforts have saved many despairing owners from the final option of having the dog destroyed, by modifying the behaviour of the dog and showing the owner how to avoid the pitfalls.

On one occasion, Lewes Crown Court in Sussex had decided that Ringo, a Labrador, should die for biting four people. But Dr Mugford's analysis and evidence to the court saved the life of the dog who was only defending his seventy-two year old master, Bill Knapp, from what the dog saw as threatening attacks. The dog was perfectly stable and provided with a halter-type nose band would no longer be a threat to anyone else.

After the case in January 1985, Dr Mugford said of the old man and the dog: 'They've only got each other. That's why they're so devoted. I'm willing to bet that if they insist on Ringo being put down, then Mr Knapp won't last long without him'.

Dr Mugford's own saintly and well adjusted Irish Setter Sam is used to help the treatment of less happy dogs. Sam, together with a younger Corgi and Dr Roger and Mrs Vivienne Mugford's four children, make a good advertisement for bringing up children and dogs together.

V

DOGS: THE BEST MEDICINE

36. *Sheila Hocken with her guide dog Emma. By a strange twist of fate, Sheila regained her sight following skilled surgery, but long-serving guide Emma became progressively blind. Emma won the devotion to duty medal in 1980.*

22. *Eyes for the blind, ears for the deaf*

Not so long ago, and certainly within my lifetime, it was quite a common sight to see pitiful blind beggars rattling their tins for money on which to live. They had no means of employment and no welfare services then.

To this day I remember one man seen many times in the Bullring in Birmingham, who always had with him a little mongrel terrier. The dog caught the eye of the stoney-hearted who might otherwise have passed by unmoved, by dancing up and down on his hind legs in a most amusing and appealing way. Then you couldn't help looking at the poor man, and guiltily dropping what you had in his tin.

Fortunately such beggars are a rare sight today, at least in Britain.

But it is only since 1931, when the Guide Dogs for the Blind Association started in England from modest beginnings in Cheshire, that an ever increasing number of people deprived of their sight have been given the marvellous new independence which a trained guide dog can provide.

It is difficult to single out just one of these wonderful dogs for a medal, but in 1980 came a nomination for a chocolate coloured Labrador called Emma, who after serving her owner faithfully for over ten years, ironically became blind herself in old age.

Sheila Hocken was the owner of Emma, and has now become well known for her vivid stories and accounts of what it is like to become increasingly blind and the difference a dog makes, in her books *Emma and I, Emma V.I.P.* and *Emma and Co.*

The first book records an extraordinary situation in which the role of blind owner and guiding dog were completely reversed. Not only did Emma lose her sight, but Sheila Hocken partially regained hers following a skilful eye operation. This was not the first time she had faced surgery, but it was the first occasion on which her sight improved as a result.

For a while after Sheila discovered that she could manage to see again, her dog Emma could also still see and her worry then was whether she would be permitted to keep Emma, the dog she had grown to love so much. The Guide Dog for the Blind Association used to officially maintain ownership of all the dogs they train. In some instances, where there is still a long period of useful guiding life in a dog, and the circumstances of the recipient change, the guide dog can be retrained quite quickly to work with another person needing a guide dog.

In view of Emma's age, Sheila was able to keep her – which was just as well when the failing eyesight of the dog started to become evident. It is so much easier for a blind dog to cope in familiar surroundings, where it knows where each piece of furniture can be found and avoided.

Emma was an apt choice to draw attention to the good work of guide dogs everywhere, and she was selected to receive a gold medal award for devotion to duty from PRO Dogs in December 1980.

At that time there were some 3000 guide dogs in Britain, but already today (1990) the number has grown further to 4000. And still the demand grows.

It must take enormous courage for a blind person to totally put trust in a dog. If you are fortunate enough to have normal vision, close your eyes and imagine what it must be like to walk forward fearlessly, into traffic and over busy roads, with your hand on the harness of a dog. It is little wonder early advocates of the idea such as Herr Johann Wilhelm Klein in Vienna in 1819 and Dr Gerhard Stalling nearly a century later in Oldenburg, West Germany, and then Mrs Dorothy Eustis the American lady who had vision to write about the scheme and its world-wide implications in 1927, found it difficult to be taken seriously. Such is the penalty paid by pioneers.

Properly trained dogs, which finally make the grade after careful selection and training have fully repaid the faith of these far-sighted people in the ability and willingness of dogs to work and please us in this most remarkable way.

The great success rate of dogs to help blind people may have helped pave the way for introducing dogs to work for people with hearing loss in America in the 1970's.

However, I keenly remember the scepticism of some when I was fortunate enough to be involved with Lady Wright and Dr Bruce Fogle in 1981 in working to introduce Hearing Dogs for the Deaf to Britain. One deaf worker was reported to be 'seething with anger' at the very idea of spending money to train dogs, and I wrote an article in an effort to refute her doubts published in *Our Dogs* in May 1982.

The scheme in Britain was launched under the auspices of the Royal National Institute for the Deaf in 1982 and became a separate charity in its own right in 1985.

But how can you train a dog to become the 'ears' of a person with hearing loss? A barking dog, warning that there is someone knocking at the door is no use if you can't hear it!

The solution is to train the dog to alert the deaf person by coming and putting a paw on the knee, or nudging him, and then going towards the source of the sound, ensuring the person follows.

In this way a dog can warn when a whistling kettle is boiling, when the alarm clock rings, when there is somebody at the door – and even fetch a deaf mother when her baby is crying.

As one in six men and one in seven women have some difficulty with hearing, and the problem worsens with age, the potential for helping large numbers of people in the future is considerable. These days life expectancy is longer and so an increasing number of people will suffer a degree of deafness in the ageing population.

The bonus in the 'hearing' dog scheme is that it can help dogs as well as people. Although fewer than a hundred dogs had been trained in Britain by 1990, most of these were selected from homes for unwanted animals.

This means that with skilful selection, a dog which might have been destroyed as unwanted, can be trained for an active life with a grateful owner.

The first dog to be trained in Britain was a retriever-type mongrel called Favour. A young dog with a white and gold coat, he had a keen expression and enjoyed the game of coming quickly to a squeaky rubber mouse, and other tests designed to test his response. This was better than kennel life, any day! He behaved perfectly. Almost as if he knew this was to be the most important event in his life.

Tony Blunt, who had never previously selected and trained a dog for this work before, was the first trainer for 'hearing' dogs in

Britain. He had spent many years training German Shepherds for the police and a few months at a centre for training 'hearing' dogs in America. This was to be quite a change and quite a challenge.

On this initial important occasion he was assisted by Pat Reilly, an American trainer from Red Acre Hearing Dog Center in Massachusetts. The Americans had a number of programmes established already, including one through the American Humane Society, and with their prior experience were most generous in sharing knowledge with us.

Favour passed his test with flying colours and said goodbye to the kennel for rejected dogs. From this day forward he was going to be wanted very much indeed. This ordinary mongrel, with a gentle nature, was destined to become a famous dog and the first success of Tony Blunt in this revolutionary programme.

The training was intensive and carried out in an unusual kennel situation. It was in the home that the dogs would have to work so these surroundings had to be provided for training. Favour learned not to bark when he heard one of the sounds he was trained to, but instead to come back and 'tell' Tony where the sound was coming from.

After four months hard work, they gave an appealing and convincing demonstration to the delight and approval of the small executive committee of Hearing Dogs for the Deaf. The scheme had worked in the U.S.A. Now we knew we could make it work in Britain, too.

Tony and Favour travelled thousands of miles all over Britain to explain, promote and demonstrate how a dog can be trained for this new work with the deaf. Favour had to work in all kind of strange, mock 'home' surroundings and even in television studios. He responded well, no matter what he was asked to do and attracted great support for the scheme.

In 1986 Favour was nominated to receive the PRO Dog gold medal award for devotion to duty, and the nomination was successful. By this time he had already given more than 1,000 demonstrations and travelled over 75,000 miles. He had been featured on the BBC television programmes *Blue Peter, Pebble Mill at One* and *John Craven's Newsround*. He was already becoming well known.

A friendly, lovable little dog, Favour was known to have one vice only – greed! Undoubtedly his favourite outings were to demonstrate to Women's Institute meetings because there he could be

39. *Each year, the celebrity gold medal winning dogs meet up again in Hyde Park, London, in May, to start the Walkover Britain fund-raising event in aid of the P.A.T. Dog Hospital Visiting Scheme. Here, the Irish wolfhound Connor, regimental mascot of the Welsh Guards, with handler Lance-Sergeant David Rutherford, joins the 1985 winners.*

appealing expression and seeming ability to charm the cameras she did her bit to create the demand for P.A.T. dogs.

Headlines such as: 'Happiness is dog-shaped,' 'Man's Best Friend can be a Healer,' 'I'm Poppy, PAT Me' and 'Canine Cure for Loneliness' gave great encouragement to the scheme.

Many of these dogs would have been worthy of consideration for a medal, including Zoe a Swedish Valhund who visited Melksham Hospital in Wiltshire to see a young man totally para-lysed after a road traffic accident. He seemed to have given up the will to live – until Zoe appeared. An unusual prescription for life-saving, but there was no better medicine the doctors could have given. The dog brought him the first renewed interest in life and he started to make a slow partial recovery. Even Sister encouraged the dog to lie on the hospital bed!

Two P.A.T. dogs, Cloe a chihuahua and Bonnie a Border terrier, were called out by different hospitals in answer to a plea for them to sit with very old ladies who were asking for them at the last moments in their lives. The friends who had given so many pleasant visits to Morden College Hospital in London and a geriatric home in Chester, were needed to just lie peacefully there, where a hand could rest on the head of the dog and give a little comfort.

These really were errands of mercy. In each case, the kindly

40. *The celebrated actress Elizabeth Quinn, who is deaf, with Favour, the first dog to be selected and trained for the Hearing Dogs for the Deaf charity in Britain.*

41. *Katie Boyle with Poppy, the English setter, one of the first dogs in Britain to be registered as a visiting P.A.T. dog, and her own Battersea Dogs' Home rescued dog, Charlie Girl.*

owner feeling fully rewarded, just by the recognition of the importance of their dog in such a situation, and in sharing dogs they loved and felt privileged to own.

The first nomination to be received for a medal for a P.A.T. dog commanded immediate attention. It was for a dog of royal breeding.

James, a Pembrokeshire corgi, was bred by H M the Queen and given to Miss Daphne Slark in 1978, ten years before the nomination was made.

Miss Slark had for many years worked as manageress at the Rozavel kennels in Pirbright, owned by the well known breeder and show judge Thelma Gray. It was this kennel which provided King George VI and Queen Elizabeth, the Queen Mother, with the first royal corgi and led to the great enthusiasm for the breed by the Queen.

Today the Queen keeps bitch puppies only, usually of the red colour which she favours and puppies are never sold but sometimes given to good permanent homes. When on one ocasion the dog puppy James was offered to Daphne Slark, he became her pride and joy.

42. *Woody the greyhound is a P.A.T. dog and has made all the difference to patients at Wandle Valley Hospital in Surrey, where he visits with his owner, Myra Hendy. Chief Nursing Officer Jean O'Shaughnessy said the visits were a huge success. 'One old gentleman, who had never spoken to us before, has started speaking since the visits began,' she said.*

43. *Singer Cliff Richard supports the P.A.T. scheme by sponsoring this Border terrier, Bonnie, belonging to Sue Holleron, one of the PRO Dogs volunteers.*

Corgis are cattle dogs, where their habit of nipping may be used to some advantage behind the cattle by the herdsmen. But the nipping does not go down so well in polite society and the press takes delight in making much of alleged incidents. Was the Right-Honourable So-and-So rounded up a little too enthusiastically by one of the diligent corgis? And did another nip a fellow member of the corgi pack in trying to establish the pecking order?

Whatever the merits of the corgis in providing copy for the press when there is nothing else to write about, it is certain that the Queen has found them to be wonderful ice-breakers on stiff and formal occasions. Then they are let loose to start people chatting and feeling more relaxed.

James had the perfectly, friendly, temperament and passed his test easily. He made regular calls to Ridgeway House, Llawhaden

44. *Miss Daphne Slark with her Welsh corgi James, bred by the Queen, who won the PRO Dog of the Year medal for pet of the year in 1988.*

in Wales where Miss Slark lived. There he gave the old folk lots to talk about and made them feel almost as if they had received a royal visit. James also made house calls on an elderly stroke patient in St Davids', providing a welcome tonic.

When Miss Slark needed a hip operation in 1988, she was pleased to find that James was permitted to visit as a registered P.A.T. dog and then it was her turn to receive the tonic.

The Queen signalled her approval of the receipt of a medal for James and sent a message to say that she remembered James 'with great affection'.

The corgi with the nippy-breed reputation, James, received his medal for pet of the year on the same night on the same stage as the German Shepherd Sammy and Max the terrier mongrel. One of the press photographers rubbed his hand with glee and confidently promised me the scrap of the year when I asked for them to be posed close for a photograph together.

But they all behaved with impeccable dignity. They had nothing to fight about. They were all top dogs. And they knew it.

DID YOU KNOW?

The Wrong Smell

One of the saddest stories told is by a widow, shortly after her husband died of cancer.

Her husband had suffered over many years and gone through all the usual harsh treatments in vogue in the 1980's, including chemotherapy. He enjoyed remissions over varying periods when he was able to return home for a while.

On his final admission to hospital in Maidstone, he became depressed and was missing his family and beloved dog very much.

One day, to cheer him up, his wife took the dog to the hospital to see him. He had not seen the dog for some months.

Sadly the dog did not know his master. The man smelt so different to the dog following the chemotherapy, and the scenting recognition is so important to the dog, that it was not possible for the dog to know that the sick man in the hospital bed was his master.

24. *Lifeline for disabled*

Jim Rigg suffered from epilepsy. It was difficult, and sometimes embarrassing when these attacks happened, but still he managed a reasonably full and normal life. He was certainly far more active in 1983 than seemed possible five years earlier, when he had been involved in a serious motor bike smash.

Jimmy's independent lifestyle was largely thanks to Tripper, his intelligent collie, purchased for a modest 50p from Singleton Park dog's home, and possibly the best investment the family ever made.

Jim and Tripper went everywhere together. Camping, walking, down to the pub, the pair were inseparable. And Jim knew he could rely on Tripper, in case of need.

In May 1983, the two set off for a walk on the beach along Pobbles Bay on Swansea's Gower coast. It was a favourite place to walk, even on the damp, blustery day which was Tuesday 22 May.

Access to the beach was difficult at high water, but when the tide was out the sandy beach was exposed and was easily reached from the adjoining cove. Few people were about in the dismal weather.

The tide was coming in fast towards the sheer rocky cliffs as the pair reached the bay and already the favourite sandy stretch was lost beneath the waves as the water rushed in towards the rocky upper foreshore. Jimmy tried to quicken his pace. He experienced the slightly odd sensation which he had learned to associate with a warning. Then, suddenly, one of the dread attacks came on and he collapsed in a seizure.

How much of the impending danger Tripper sensed we shall never know. The natural instinct of the protective dog would be to stay with his owner. Perhaps Tripper did this for a while. The dog knew the coast well, but is a dog able to sum up intelligently the danger of a man in this situation?

Whatever the reason, the dog then did a remarkable thing. It seems that somehow he knew he had to go and get help for Jim.

45. *Tripper the Welsh collie who saved the life of his owner, Jim Rigg, won the PRO Dog medal for life-saving in 1983, presented by Jilly Cooper.*

He raced off until he found a group of holidaymakers half a mile away in some chalets at the far end of the beach at Three Cliffs Bay. He whined and barked and it was obvious to them that the dog was very agitated about something. But what?

Tripper continued to whine, running to and fro until they realised he wanted them to follow him, which eventually they did.

When they found Jim he was still unconscious and they immediately ran to alert the coast guard station and ambulance crew. Soon it was obvious that the emergency helicopter would also have to be called out.

Winchman Sergeant Dick Crocker, reported by David Newman of the *Daily Star*, said: 'When I went down the wire, the ambulancemen were treating Jim and the dog was sitting on the guy's legs.

'There was no way he wanted to leave his master. In the end we had to physically lift the dog off the man's legs. I think he wanted to come up in the chopper too.'

Jim was taken to Singleton hospital in Swansea were his condition was described as fairly comfortable. But he was detained for four days to recover from the unpleasant and serious attack he had suffered.

Meanwhile the worried Tripper who had watched frantically as his beloved owner was winched up through the air on a wire, was taken back home by neighbours. He was very distressed and as soon as the back door was left open for a moment, he dashed back to the spot where he had last seen Jim.

By this time, the water covered the rocks and a short time later the dog was seen frantically swimming about in the water. He was again taken home, where he was kept safely in the house until happily reunited with Jim four days later.

It was generally agreed by the rescuers that Jim certainly owed his life to eight year old Tripper.

Mrs Wright, Jim's mother said later from their home in Hael Lane, Pennard: 'I don't know what my son would do without Tripper. He is quite independent, but that dog is his lifeline.'

And then she revealed that just four months earlier, Tripper had also come to Jim's aid. They had been walking together in a country lane some way from home when Jim had suffered a typical blackout attack.

On that occasion it was raining, and Tripper had lain over Jim's unconscious body to protect him from the wet, cold, February day, barking to attract attention when he heard people approaching, until help came.

In May 1983, as he was photographed with his happy dog, Jim said gratefully: 'There's no secret about it. He's my best pal and he looks after me like a brother'.

Later that year, proud Jim and family came to London, and Tripper was honoured with the 1983 gold medal award for life saving. Throughout the evening the dog's devotion to Jim was obvious for all to see. His eyes never left his master and he responded to his every move, without a single command, almost as if he was an extension of Jim's will. When Jim stood up, the dog was immediately on his feet, and when the young man sat, Tripper lay beside him. It was the kind of response that obedience fanatics spend years trying to achieve. An all too rare natural partnership that comes through mutual understanding.

In updating my research for this book, I learned that Tripper lived to the age of fourteen years and died in September 1989.

Although, for Jim, no dog will ever replace Tripper, the good news is that he does have another dog and his attacks of epilepsy have become less frequent over the years.

Many people, far more physically handicapped than Jim, have found through experience that dogs can be useful to them. Dogs learn readily how to retrieve, fetch and return things which people who cannot stoop are unable to reach for themselves.

This idea was taken an important step further in America in 1975 by Bonita Bergin, who founded an organisation called Canine Companions for Independence. In this scheme, dogs are carefully selected and trained to do collect-and-carry tasks. They also learn to use light and elevator switches and to follow a wheelchair without being on a lead. The dogs are then matched with a needy handicapped person who is willing and able to care for the dog and provide a rewarding life style for the dog, in return for the devoted service which the dog is trained to give.

None of the cruel electric-shock reinforcement used to train some monkeys to become the slaves of the disabled are needed, or can ever be justified, in training animals to help people.

Anyone wishing to benefit from an animal trained to work to assist them should first satisfy themselves that the animal has been kindly and sympathetically treated in training. Even in the show ring, or obedience competition ring, it has been known for dogs occasionally to be deprived of food or water for hours – and then offered a small titbit or drop of water in an effort to extort a keener performance.

Such methods never deserve to succeed and are the weapons of inadequate trainers who have failed to awaken the natural willing response of the happy, intelligent dog.

Melissa, an appealing child born with muscular distrophy, and confined to a wheelchair, has been used with huge success to promote Canine Companions for Independence in California.

The day starts for Melissa when Cashew, her happy golden retriever, reaches up and gently places a paw on her shoulder to awaken her – and then rushes off to find her slippers and deliver them to her lap. Throughout the day, the dog works happily to retrieve dropped crayons and papers, fetch her shoes and hair ribbons and accompanies her every journey in the wheelchair.

The scheme aims to train exceptional dogs for exceptional people and is the forerunner of the similar SOHO-Foundation in Holland.

SOHO, founded in 1984, claims to be the first such programme in Europe, and their reasonably 'local' expertise was called upon when Assistance Dogs for Disabled People started in England in March 1987. I was glad to be asked to attend this inaugural meeting held at the Kennel Club in London, which actually resulted in the formation of two groups set up with similar aims.

Anne Conway, a long established supporter of PRO Dogs, who became well known by fund-raising for Hearing Dogs for the Deaf when her appealing self-trained cocker spaniels Lucy and Charlie Brown, took the helm of Assistance Dogs for Disabled People, based in the South of England. Frances Day, who had a leg amputated due to bone cancer as a child, and was keenly aware of the problems caused by such a handicap, formed Dogs for the Disabled in the Midlands, which trained its first two dogs in 1988.

But while it is true in the main that properly trained dogs are able to perform far more in the way of helpful tasks than the untrained, many family pets have saved the lives of their owners just through their natural protective instincts. Disabled people can especially benefit.

A good illustration of this is Judy, a Jack Russell type dog who saved the life of her seventy four year old crippled owner when fire broke out at his bungalow home in Newhall in the Midlands on the night of 28 June 1984. The eleven year old dog alerted Mr Joseph Bennett to the danger by doing something totally out of character and the report made front page news in the *Burton Mail* next day.

'I was in the bathroom at about 7 p.m. when Judy started whining and tapping on the door. She has never done anything like that before and she is not allowed in that part of the house. The wife never allowed her in the bedroom or in the passage outside the bathroom,' he explained.

When Mr Bennett came out of the bathroom he found smoke seeping round the living-room door. He went into the room and found flames licking up the side of the settee. A cigarette left on the edge of the ashtray was responsible for the blaze.

Joseph Bennett, who was crippled by polio when he was four years old, and left unable to stand or walk, made frantic but unsuccessful attempts to put out the blaze with water carried from the kitchen in his wheelchair.

Suddenly there was a bang as the windows went, and flames were everywhere. The back door was jammed and it seemed as if Mr Bennett and Judy would perish in the dreadful heat. At last the door was freed and they made their escape.

Judy's frantic barking had alerted the neighbours before the flames became obvious, and Mrs Elsie Yeomans from across the road came to push the wheelchair to safety.

There was no time to save Joey the budgie, who died in the fire. Joey was Judy's pal. Nothing he liked better than to perch on the table by the dog. The bird had learned to bark like a dog – a trick self-taught by imitating Judy.

Mr and Mrs Bennett lost all their possessions and the bungalow was gutted. There is little doubt that without Judy's warning, Mr Bennett would have been trapped and unable to escape in time.

'Judy's a good friend to me,' said Joseph Bennett proudly when he came to London with his dog to receive the 1984 PRO Dog of the year gold medal award for life-saving. 'We have great drives in my invalid car. There's just room for the two of us. And now she's saved my life. What more can a good dog do?'

In the future, as understanding grows about the importance of the lifeline which trained dogs in particular can provide in bringing greater freedom and independence to disabled people, it is certain that the demand will grow.

With it should come a growing respect by society for the benefits provided by such wonderful, friendly and willing helpers.

Too much money has been spent by those who seek curbs on where man and dog are welcome together, in trying to calculate the cost to society of the damage done by unwanted dogs. This is the fault of people who allow unwanted dogs to be born and permit an irresponsible easy-come, easy-go attitude to taking on the lifelong commitment of caring dog ownership. It is certainly not the fault of dogs themselves.

But how can we realistically calculate the enormous debt which we owe to dogs? What equation would be needed to cost the benefits in terms of well-being, loss of loneliness, savings to the health service by helping keep people fit in mind and body – and out of hospital? And what about the lifeline provided by so many dogs to more disabled people?

Like true human friendship, the value is beyond price.

DID YOU KNOW?

Black Death Scapegoat

Too often dogs are made a convenient scapegoat when things go wrong. It is an unpleasant fact that insensitive people, unable to defend themselves, will sometimes take revenge by kicking an innocent dog, when things go wrong in life. Dogs suffer in silence and do not answer back.

One of the most terrifying ills to befall mankind in past history was the plague, or Black Death, which caused 10,000 human deaths a day at its height.

During the Tudor period in England there were repeated outbreaks of the dread Black Death. There was no cure and doctors were at their wit's end, as was Parliament, to try to contain the disease. Action of some kind was needed, and sacrifice demanded. The dog provided a scapegoat and cats were sacrified too.

The plague order decreed that the sign of the cross should be set on every house affected, that no sick person should go out for one month and that dogs should be killed. Dogs of noblemen, including hounds, spaniels and mastiffs were spared, but had to be confined to quarters.

The only people to prosper in these dreadful times were the grave-diggers coffin makers and dog killers. The rats went free and it was not until the 1890's that the link between rats, rat fleas and the plague in man was discovered.

Dogs are incapable of transmitting the plague directly to people and the mass sacrifice was in vain.

25. Dogs to detect cancer?

Through the pages of this book it will have become increasingly clear that in the last fifty years our eyes have opened wider towards many new ways in which dogs are able to help people.

Even a century ago, the idea that a blind person could totally trust his (or her) life to a guide dog would have been unthinkable. As for P.A.T. dogs on hospital wards, 'hearing' dogs to assist people who are deaf, or assistance dogs to allow people confined to wheelchairs to lead fuller more independent lives – all this would have rated as extreme fringe medicine which would not catch on. But those who have placed their trust in the friendly cooperative instincts of the dog have rarely been disappointed, and demand for all these new groups of companionable dogs is increasing rapidly all the time, as more recognise their advantages.

The dog is ever willing to please and to adapt to the changing needs of man, and much prefers to be actively involved in the life of his owner than confined to unbearable hours of boredom, in confined premises while his family is out all day.

There seems no doubt that of all the splendid animals living in the world, none is more able and willing to share our lifestyle and deserving of the title, 'man's best friend', than the dog.

But what of the future? Can there be ways, as yet glimpsed only by the far-sighted, where dogs may be able to save man from any of the biggest killers, filling our hospitals today?

Following a letter published in *The Lancet* by Dr Hywel Williams and Mr Andrew Pembroke of the Department of Dermatology, King's College Hospital, London on 1 April 1989, a most unusual nomination for a Pet of the Year medal was sent to PRO Dogs, by an observant member of their medical panel.

The letter in *The Lancet* explained that a forty-four year old woman had been referred to the clinic at the hospital with a mole on her left thigh. But it is the story of what made this patient seek treatment in the first place which should stir public and medical interest.

The facts are these.

When two year old Border collie × dobermann, Boo, started to sniff at the back of Mrs Bonita Whitfield's leg, she told her to go away and stop being a nuisance. But the dog was constantly attracted to the same spot, and Mrs Whitfield investigated to see what was causing the interest.

She found a mole which she had not been aware of previously, which was about the size of a thumbnail. But still thought nothing of it.

Boo continued her interest, sniffing insistently through clothing whenever she got the chance, much to Mrs Whitfield's annoyance. The dog took no notice of any other moles. The ritual continued for several months and culminated in the dog trying to nibble the lesion off one day when Mrs Whitfield wore shorts.

At last this prompted Mrs Whitfield to go to her doctor. He referred her to King's College Hospital, where it was decided necessary to remove the suspicious looking mole at once. Histological examination confirmed this to be a malignant melanoma but because it had been removed at the thin and curable stage it caused very little inconvience and was successfully and completely removed.

Dr Hywel Williams, registrar in dermatology, is very concerned about the world-wide growing incidence of skin cancer and carefully monitors all cases referred to his department. His research project led him to examine very carefully the case notes for Mrs Whitfield and as a man who always enjoyed the company of dogs in general, and beagles in particular, he was immediately interested in Boo's contribution.

As he was driving home in his car after reading the notes, the possible full significance of the contribution by the dog slowly dawned on him. Clearly Boo's sniffing, and the potential power of the highly developed scenting ability of other pet dogs, might be responsible for saving human life by early detection of growths giving off a distinctive odour.

In his letter to the *Lancet*, Dr Williams put forward the suggestion that malignant tumours may emit unique odours which, though undetectable to man, are easily detected by dogs. More work in this area might be expected to confirm either that benign

46. *Mrs Bonita Whitfield with her dog Boo who saved her life by detecting her skin cancer at an early stage. Boo won the 1989 medal for life-saving at the annual canine 'Oscar' presentations ceremony.*

tumours give off no odour at all, or that the scent of these 'safe' growths cause no curiosity to the nose of the dog.

Dr Williams says that although they 'have not yet proceeded to a trial of sniffer dogs in the melanoma clinic,' the adjunctive use of such animals is worth serious consideration. He then endears himself at once to animal lovers everywhere by saying that testing this theory would be much more useful than using beagles to study tobacco carcinogenises.

The exposé of the horrific way in which the gentle and obliging beagle dogs were strapped down in laboratories and forced to inhale cigarette smoke, will never be forgotten by those who care about misuse of animals. How could such an experiment ever be justified to test the curiosity of scientists as to how many weeks of enforced smoking dogs might have to endure before developing signs of lung cancer? (In fact, once again, animals proved an incomparable model, and did not react in the same way as people. In any case, it is of course impossible to exactly match the elements and circumstances met by the average human smoker, in a laboratory.) All this suffering, in a futile effort to make man's self-chosen and foolish addiction to tobacco perfectly safe.

Publication of Dr Williams' letter had several beneficial effects. It not only led to recognition of Boo's contribution by presentation of the PRO Dog of the Year gold medal as pet of the year 1989, but also resulted in correspondence from Canada and Universities in Britain interested in offering information and testing the theory further.

If we are to use dogs again for human benefit, let us ensure that the law-makers and the scientists remember that it can only be justified provided the dogs themselves are not abused. Indeed, dogs working to help people deserve a particularly good and rewarding lifestyle and to be given only work and activities which they themselves enjoy. Research which deprives dogs of a good, companionable environment, which they crave, should never be permitted.

Surely the way in which we can gain most from the insight by Dr Hywel Williams, is to use the machine of publicity? This is what the gold medal award helped to achieve. When dog owners are alert to the facts, dogs can provide this extra useful function while living their normal life with their owners.

We should all be grateful for the public spirited permission which Mrs Whitfield was kind enough to give when I was researching this story, for needless to say, her name was not included in the letter to *The Lancet* and it was necessary for her to reveal herself and step into the limelight with Boo in order to receive the medal with due acclaim.

Although Mrs Whitfield was at first not too keen for her personal details to be made public, she agreed in the interests of hope for future benefits from the theory and to celebrate yet another way in which dogs may be able to help people – when their owners become aware of what mole-sniffing may mean.

Bibliography

Anderson, R.S., ed. *Pet Animals and Society*, published for the British Small Animal Veterinary Association, London: Baillière Tindall, 1975

Andrews, Michael, *The Life that Lives on Man*: Faber and Faber 1976

Bower, John and David Youngs, *The Health of Your Dog*: Crowood Press, 1989

Coombe, Iris, *Herding Dogs*: Faber and Faber, 1987

Dogs' Home Battersea, *A Passion for Dogs*: David & Charles, October 1990.

Hall, Rebecca, *Voiceless Victims*: Wildwood House, 1984

Halstock, Max, *Rats the Story of a Dog Soldier*: Victor Gollancz, 1981

Fiennes, Ranulph and Virginia *Bothie the Polar Dog*: Hodder and Stoughton, 1984

Locke, Angela, *Search Dog*: Sphere Books, 1988

Lorenz, Konrad, *Man Meets Dog* (translated by Marjorie Kerr Wilson) Baltimore: Penguin, 1953

Messent, Peter, *Understanding Your Dog*: Macdonald and Jane's

Morris, Desmond, *Dogwatching*: Jonathan Cape, 1986

Patmore, Angela, *The Mongrel*: Popular Dogs, Century-Hutchinson, 1985

Porter, Valerie, *The Guinness Book of Almost Everything You Didn't Need to Know about Dogs*: Guinness Superlatives, 1986

Proceedings of Vth International Conference on the Relationship Between Humans and Animals, AFIRAC – Association Francaise d'Information et de Recherche sur l'Animal de Compagnie, Monaco November 15–18, 1989

Proceedings of International Symposium on the Human–Pet Relationship, IEMT – Institute for Interdisciplinary Research on the Human–Pet Relationship, ed. Austrian Academy of Sciences, Vienna, October 27–28, 1983

Scott-Ordish, Lesley, *Your Dog, Without You*: PRO Dogs National Charity, Maidstone, Kent, U.K., 1989

Serpell, James, *In the Company of Animals*: Basil Blackwell, 1986

Salk, Lee, *Raising Better Children*: Pets Are Wonderful Council, Chicago, USA, 1985

Useful Addresses

PROTECTING ANIMALS/DOGS

Animal Aid*
7 Castle Street
Tonbridge
Kent
TN9 1BH
(Founder: Jean Pink 1977)

Animal Health Trust
PO Box 5
Snailwell Road
Newmarket
Suffolk
CB8 7DW

Animal Welfare Trust
Tylers Way
Watford By Pass
Watford
Herts
WD2 8HQ

The Blue Cross
Animals Hospital
1 Hugh Street
London
SW1V 1RP

The Dogs Home Battersea
4 Battersea Park Road
London
SW8 4AA

Holly Blood Donor Appeal*
PO Box 95
Dartford
Kent
DA1 1UE
(Founder: Harry Hibben 1989)

Last Chance Animal Rescue*
Stickhill
Edenbridge
Kent
(Founder: Sylvia Wragg 1977)

Peoples Dispensary for Sick Animals
PDSA Head Office
Whitechapel Way
Priorslee
Telford, Shropshire
TF2 9PQ

* These organisations all originated in the County of Kent, U.K.

PRO Dogs National Charity*
National Head Office
Rocky Bank
New Road
Ditton, Aylesford, Kent
ME20 6AD
(Founder: Lesley   Scott-
Ordish 1976)

Pine Ridge Dog Sanctury
Priory Road
Ascot
Berkshire
SL5 8RJ

**Wood Green Animal
  Shelters**
Highway Cottage
Chishill Road
Heydon
Nr Royston, Herts
SG8 8PN

PROVIDING DOGS TO HELP PEOPLE (UK)

**Assistance Dogs for
  Disabled People**
23 Slipper Road
Emsworth
Hampshire
PO10 8BS

Dogs for the Disabled
Brook House
1 Lower Ladyes Hills
Kenilworth
Warwickshire
CV8 2GN

**The Guide Dogs for the
  Blind Association**
Alexandra House
Park Street
Windsor
Berkshire
SL14 1JR

Hearing Dogs for the Deaf
Training Centre
London Road (A40
Lewknor
Oxford
OX9 5RY

* Originated in the County of Kent, U.K.

Dogs visiting hospitals, with their owners

Pets As Therapy (PAT)*
Incorporating PAT Dogs
Rocky Bank
New Road
Ditton, Aylesford, Kent
ME20 6AD

Dogs searching, with thier owners

Search & Rescue Dog Association
SARDA
Greenstones
Old Hall Road
Troutbeck Bridge
Windemere
Cumbria

PROVIDING DOGS TO HELP PEOPLE (Overseas)

American Humane Association
Hearing Dog Programme
1500 West Tufts Avenue
Englewood, Colorado 80111
USA

Red Acre Farm
Hearing Dog Centre
Stow
Massachusetts 01775
USA

Trained dogs for disabled people (other than the blind)

**Canine Companions for
  Independence**
PO Box 446
1221 Sabastopol Road
Santa Rosa
CA 95402

Sftichting SOHO
Kloosterstraat 7
5373 AG Herpen
Holland

* Originated in the County of Kent, U.K.

National Guide Dog organisations, outside the U.K.

Sftichting Koninkiljk Nederlands Geleidenhonden Fonds
Postbus 544
1180 AM Amstelveen
Holland

Royal Guide Dogs Assn., of Australia
Chandlers Highway
Kew
3101 Victoria
Australia

Seeing Eye Inc.
Morristown
New Jersey
07963 – 0375
USA

STUDYING THE IMPORTANCE OF ANIMALS (U.K.)

Association of Pet Behaviour Consultants
50 Pall Mall
London
SW1

Society of Companion Animals Studies
The Mews Cottage
7 Botanic Crescent Lane
Glasgow
G20 8AA

David Cavill
Canine Studies Institute
London Road
Bracknell
Berkshire
RG12 6QN

Companion Animal Behaviour Studies Group
Department of Biology
University of Southampton
Southampton
Hampshire
SO9 3TU

Studying the Importance of Animals (Overseas)

AFIRAC
Association Francaise D'Information et de Recherche sur L'animal de Compagnie
7 Rue du Pasteur Wagner
75011 Paris, France

Delta Society
PO Box 1080
Renton
WA 98057
USA

**Center for Interaction of
  Animals and Soceity**
School of Veterinary Medicine
University of Pennsylvania
Philadelphia, PA
USA

**Institute for Interdisciplinary
  Research on the Human–Pet
  Relationship**
Weyringergasse 28A
A-1040 Vienna
Austria

OTHER USEFUL ADDRESSES IN THE U.K.

DNA genetic fingerprinting to establish parentage of puppies from a
  bitch mated by more than one dog:

University Hospital of Wales
Heath Park
Cardiff
CF4 4XW

Grief counselling to cope with distress on death of a dog. Also
  arrangements for care of a dog after the death of the owner (limited to
members):

PRO Dogs National Charity*
Rocky Bank
New Road
Ditton, Maidstone
Kent
ME20 6AD

Governing body of pedigree dogs in the U.K. Also Crufts dog show:

The Kennel Club
1–5 Clarges Street
Piccadilly
London
W1Y 8AB

* Originated in the County of Kent, U.K.

Leading animal behaviourist with safe toys and kindly control devices:

Dr Roger Mugford
The Company of Animals
PO Box 23
Chertsey
Surrey
KT16 0PU

Major dog show for mongrelss:

Scruffts*
Hewitts Farm
A224
Orpington
Kent
(Alex Bruce 1983)

REGULAR READING ABOUT DOGS IN THE U.K.

Argos
Pro Dogs National Charity
Rocky Bank
New Road
Ditton, Aylesford
Kent
ME20 6AD

Dogs Monthly
Bowen Industrial Estate
Aberbagoed
Bargoed
Mid Glamorgan
CF8 9ET

Dog World
9 Tufton Street
Ashford
Kent
TN23 1QN

Dog Training Weekly
Penrhiw Club
Letterston
Haverfordwest
Dyfed
SA62 5BW

* Originated in the County of Kent, U.K.

Kennel Gazette
The Kennel Club
1–5 Clarges Street
PIccadilly
London
W1A 8AB

Obedience Competitor
Long Meadows
Mooredges, Thorne
Doncaster
South Yorkshire
DN8 5RY

Our Dogs
Oxford Road Station
    Approach
Manchester
M60 1SX

Working Trials Monthly*
16 Hartlip Hill
Hartlip
Nr Sittingbourne
Kent
ME9 7PA
(J & B Harvey 1986)

Pet Dogs
PO Box 26F
Chessington
Surrey
KT9 1DN

You and Your Vet
7 Mansfield Street
London
W1M 0AT

* Originated in the County of Kent, U.K.

Index

Numbers shown in parentheses refer to numbered photographic illustrations